WHEN WE FREE
THE WORLD

KEVIN POWELL

kepo Inc.
49 Flatbush Avenue
Suite 1024
Brooklyn, New York 11217

in an exclusive ebook partnership with Apple Books

Apple Books ebook edition June 2020

For information about special discounts for bulk orders of paperback, ebook, or audio book,
please contact kevin@kevinpowell.net

Manufactured in the United States of America

10 9 8 7 6 5 4 3 2 1

Library of Congress Cataloging-in-Publication Data is available.

ISBN 978-1-7351997-2-6 (paperback)

ISBN 978-1-7351997-1-9 (ebook)

ISBN 978-1-7351997-0-2 (audio book)

For Ellison Marcellus Garnes,
genius child, dope human being, free person he will be–

I wish I knew how it would feel to be free
I wish I could break all the chains holding me....
—NINA SIMONE singing the song created by BILLY TAYLOR

"...what I've learned is that freedom comes when you tell your story;
freedom comes when you tell the truth."
—EVE ENSLER

TABLE OF CONTENTS

A PREFACE

I am an artist, a writer, a man, a son, a husband, a human being, a very imperfect and very fragile person. And I love people, all people, no matter who they are, no matter what they call themselves. But the suffering that I experienced in these various aspects of my life in the year 2018, from people, every sort of people, compelled me to write this book. My peace of mind, and, indeed, my life, depended on it—that is how bad things had fallen apart. I brought that sense of urgency and of necessity to this task. The first draft of this book—in its entirety—spewed from me in a mere three weeks. I needed to speak, to be heard, to write, to tell my story in my way, for the sake of my sanity, for the sake of my soul. The horrific things that I experienced in one 12-month period seared me like a branding iron. You see, writing, the art form that I began practicing as a youth, heals me both spiritually and emotionally.

I know that words matter, that books and blogs and poems and plays and other kinds of writing matter, because writing saved me, empowered me, changed me, and gave me a sense of higher purpose. From my first published article 30 years ago through my 14 books, people have told me that something I wrote helped them... moved them... caused them to reconsider their most deeply held beliefs and self-perceptions. That motivates me to put words on the page, with complete honesty. I cannot write any other way than as a truth-teller, even when doing so causes me—or others—frustration, discomfort, and sadness. Those who see themselves as artists seek freedom... to be free... to be our best selves... to tell our stories in the manner that we want to tell them, without any interference from others. We must be the authors of our lives, not anyone else.

My multiple roles as leader, activist, community organizer, public servant or helper to others, and artist often put me in a compromising and a humbling position. Artists and activists, throughout history, find themselves misunderstood, ridiculed, and attacked. I accept that as part and parcel of the path I follow, and I expect to be the object of racist and demeaning assaults. No matter, with minimal resources, I continue to do my work. I seek neither sympathy nor pity. In fact, I ask for nothing at all other than to pursue the life I chose—or what the

Christian tradition views as the life to which I was "called." I remain the poor Black boy born and raised in an American ghetto many years back and see myself, this nation, and our planet, through the lens of those who have been forgotten or left out, who have been made to feel invisible and powerless. At this stage of my life, I know that I hold power and that I am visible, most importantly, to myself.

That will never change, regardless of the blessings I hold dear and the tension between who I was and who I am now. Yes, this is my fourteenth book, both a gift and a miracle to me, given that I am the son of a mother with a grade-school education and of a grandmother who could neither read nor write. I write for them... for me... for all those who feel that no one hears their voices. Likewise, I live my life out loud, as an open book, and I do the things that people told me I could never do, or should not do, because I will never be a prisoner to someone else's fears or lack of courage. I have traveled to all 50 American states and 5 of the 7 continents in this world because of my life work as an activist, as a writer, as a public speaker. That same poor Black child from Jersey City, New Jersey, made those journeys because he dared to believe, long ago, that he could live a life of passion and purpose, if he could only learn to love himself, to trust himself, to push back, even when it hurts bad, the thousand traumas of his fragile life, to believe in that word freedom and what it could mean for him as if his very life depended on it, because it does–

The pursuit of freedom brought my mother and my Aunt Birdie and my Aunt Cathy from the backwoods of the Low Country of South Carolina to New Jersey. Barely out of their teens, they stuffed their meager belongings into cheap suitcases after working hard in the homes of well-to-do White folks to save the coins to buy Greyhound bus tickets. Like their cousins before them, they traveled to the place where I would be born. They did not know what awaited them as they–three young Black women–shook off the burdens of racism, of sexism, of classism, and watched their new lives begin as that bus passed through South Carolina, North Carolina, Virginia, Washington, D.C., Maryland, Delaware, and finally arrived in North Jersey. They survived without the #MeToo movement, Black Lives Matter, or therapy or healing circles or retreats or yoga classes or candles and incense and meditation sessions. They relied on each other and their prayers for better lives than those they escaped. They could not know what awaited them as they squeezed their bodies into the same bed in the same room of a rooming house for people looking for freedom, and a new path–just like them. They could not know what awaited them as they went to work, as poor Black women, in the homes of well-to-do White folks, in the back-breaking factories, to make a way out of no way. And there is no way they could have known upon their arrival, that of the three sisters, only one, my Aunt Birdie, would never stop looking for freedom, would never stop looking for herself.

My mother and my Aunt Cathy lost vast parts of their lives due to circumstances beyond their control. Both conceived sons, my cousin Anthony and I, within two years of their arrival in the promised land of the North, with my cousin being born only three days apart from me in the same month and the same year. Aunt Birdie would not have a child for years to come, which allowed her to keep going, to keep seeking, to keep being free. The men my mother and Aunt Cathy met, the love they thought these men bestowed upon them, stripped away whatever freedom they had gained simply by leaving the South for a better life. They became enslaved anew by urban poverty and fear and confusion on how to raise their boy children; they became enslaved anew by the insanity of life inside of an American ghetto, not clear how to get out, not clear how to be free, life an assembly line of welfare, food stamps, government cheese, rats, roaches, heatless apartments, and corrupt landlords and corrupt preachers. They did the best they could with what they had, to raise and protect my cousin Anthony and me from the abuses of this world. They loved and bathed us in their own ways, and I now believe, these multiple lifetimes later, that my mother and Aunt Cathy understood, somewhere in the lighter moments of the heavy loads they carried, that we achieve freedom's highest purpose when we free someone else, even if we never succeed in freeing ourselves. My mother put me on her shoulders and taught me to see and think things she would never experience for herself. My mother told me at age three that I would go to college, although she had never set foot on a college campus, although there were no books in our home in those early days, except for the Bible. My mother took me to a library in Jersey City, the Greenville Branch, and that first visit changed my life forever, because I instantly fell in love with the magic of words, with the allure of books, with, well, being free. I remain that eight-year-old boy roaming the cavernous stacks of that massive-to-my-eyes library yearning to read, yearning to be free—

For that reason, I chose freedom as the topic for this book. My mother has never traveled on a plane, rarely leaves Jersey City, except for occasional trips back to our family homeland of South Carolina via bus or train, or one recent occasion when my wife and I drove her and my Aunt Cathy back to the soil that birthed them. Like me, my Aunt Birdie has taken planes many times, and has sought freedom however she can, on her terms. I do not judge anyone, and I understand how fear, and violence, and division, and hate, within us, toward each other, can limit any human being, can easily pit human beings against themselves, against each other. I also understand that my mother and my Aunt Cathy are free in their own way, as they lived the best lives that they could with their limited resources. Retired now, they reside in the same senior facility, in a slow-motion space with no debt, leading humble lives. They do things that they want to do in the way they want to do them. They live their lives on their own terms. I overstand those who believe that we achieve true freedom by keeping things very simple, very practical, for ourselves and for those with whom we interact. I take great pleasure, more than ever, in the basic aspects of life, as my mother and my Aunt Cathy do. I have witnessed numerous acts of compassion and caring in my lifetime... as well as an abundance of displays of meanness and greed and a recklessness toward other human beings. I relish each act of human kindness that I encounter, and I suffer gravely with the ugliness and inhumanity and disrespect that I experience. I know that we in America, and on this Earth—are a traumatized human race... the tragic legacy of the history of our country and of the world. One need only consider all the wars and other acts of physical, verbal, mental, and spiritual violence that we inflict upon each other coupled with the disdain heaped upon those who seek nothing more than to be truth-tellers, to be healers, to be bridge-builders instead of bridge-destroyers, to examine themselves, their families, their communities, their souls, their minds, their hearts. I reflected on all of this as I wrote this book and decided to call it *When We Free The World*, and to include a multi-cultural and multi-identity group of young people on the cover. They represent hope and endless possibilities, they represent the best of who we have been, who we are, if we never let the curious inner child or the youthful fearlessness inside of us die. Yes, the changes we need in America—and in this world—must come from us all, we the people, younger people, older people, everyday people who lead everyday lives.

This drives me every day now, more than ever, as I write, as I create art, as I speak, as I continue to be a leader, an activist, a servant to others. What do the words free and freedom mean to me and for me, what does it mean and what can it mean for others, in the face of the treacherous roads we travel? Yes, I shed tears often thinking about the ups and downs of my own life—personally and professionally—and it pains me to watch the world turn, again and again, toward madness and self-destruction. Through it all, love, faith, hope, and the mightily protective armor of my ancestors sustain me and convince me that better days lie ahead... for my mother and my aunts and my family... for every member of the human family... and, yes, for me. I awaken each day with a renewed sense of the great things that can be achieved by those who are truly free, by those who truly want to be free, despite anything that has happened in the past—

LETTER TO MY UNBORN CHILD

I honestly do not know where to begin, because these are very harsh and frightening times... times so harsh and frightening that I have openly wondered—as my mother used to say to me when I was a boy—if I am going to make it. Please do not get me wrong. There is happiness, here, there is hope, here, there are small victories here... there... everywhere. I am married, for one, to a brilliant and beautiful woman, Jinah Parker, and for that I am eternally blessed. I still get to do my work as a writer, as a public speaker, as an activist and servant and helper to others. And I still get to travel a great deal, to places I've been, to places I've never been, which in and of itself has helped me, has healed me in ways I could not even begin to say.

But, my child, I would be lying to you if I also did not say that these years in which we live have also nearly destroyed me on a few occasions, at times strained my marriage, my partnership with my wife, and made me question, too, why I am alive. Additionally, my mother has been ill for the past couple of years, and that weighs on me mightily. As you more than likely will be, I am an only child, the only child of my ma, so the heavy burden of caring for her as she struggles with severe pain in the form of diabetes, high blood pressure, and arthritis, falls squarely on me. It does not help that my mother —as powerful and intelligent as she is—is also savagely injured from all the things she has experienced in America, from the moment of her birth. My mother is stuck, very much so, on another mental plane, in another era, and I inherit, completely naked and completely defenseless, the weight and body blows of the rage she has for anything and anyone she feels—real or imagined—has given her the middle finger repeatedly, because she is Black, because she is poor, because she is a woman. There is no other way to say this. And as her child, one who has sought love and comfort from her my entire life, I cannot begin to tell you how much it still shocks and paralyzes me every single time my mother screams or calls me a name—a curse word—because she has no other vocabulary to express the bottomless hurt of all she continues to endure. Her body has broken down because the world has broken my mother. Yes, when people are hurt, when people are emotionally damaged, they transfer that hurt, that damage, to others, to loved ones—husbands, wives, partners, family members, co-workers, strangers, and, yes, to their children. That is why I am writing this letter to you, my unborn child. I do not want to transfer my sorrow songs or my many traumas to you. The cycles must be broken, I so desperately want to heal, I so desperately want to be different. This is why I have spent endless years in therapy, and why I am back there again because, frankly, I need it. Old patterns have resurfaced that I am not proud of—

So, I write this letter to you, to your soul, to your heart, because I do not even know if my wife and I will ever have you, if we will ever produce a child. I want you, I do want a child, badly, because I so badly want to do for you what my mother and my absent father were never able to do for me. I want to tell you I love you from the minute you are conceived. I want to hold and hug and kiss you, no matter your gender identity, at every opportunity. I want to make you feel safe, yes, but I also want to tell you the truth, the whole truth, about America, about this world, because you will be Black like me, and you will sing the blues as I have sung the blues, from the very moment you begin to realize that so much of this world does not love or respect or honor you, or most of us who have skin like yours. I have felt this hate and sadness and alienation since I was a child, since I was a youth myself. It began when I was attending Public School 38 in my hometown of Jersey City, New Jersey, and I could not understand why a group of older White boys showed up one day, with fists tightly balled, and with rocks and bricks and bottles and God knows what else in their hands, and threatened to attack us Black and Latinx children, just because of who we were, as we stood, trembling, on the other side of the school fence. It frightened me, terribly, and I would never forget this group, they were called the BONES, which stood for "Beat On N****rs Every Second." We kids were only about eight or nine years old. The police came, the angry mob scattered, but I can see the contorted faces and the contorted bodies of those angry White boys as clear as day this very second. Only a few years later, my mother and Aunt Cathy made the monumental decision to move us to a majority White neighborhood in Jersey City, presumably to save my cousin Anthony and me and our mothers from the messy and wholly violent web of the ghetto, and within days, while attempting to play stickball with the White boys on the block, one casually and repeatedly called me "n****r" like it was no big deal, until I chased him, in tears, with the stick we were using to hit the ball, right to his doorsteps. And a mere two years after that, when I was fifteen years old, I would get into a fight, as boys often do, with a Puerto Rican kid, as we rode on a city bus after school. The bus driver panicked, and he called the cops. The Puerto Rican boy, who had fair skin and was much lighter than me, was gently escorted off the bus to a police car. The other officer literally threw me off the bus and handcuffed me. Once in the back of the squad car I noted the Puerto Rican boy smiling upfront, not handcuffed at all. I protested, loudly, the big White male cop next to me told me to shut my mouth, I said "No," and other choice words, and he then methodically smashed and bloodied my nose with one punch. My puny body slumped in that back seat, I saw stars before my eyes, I sobbed uncontrollably as the red liquid from my nostrils filled the front of my light beige winter jacket. I think back on it now, often—that singular incident—and I realize that the cop could have killed me, as many of us have been murdered through the years by police officers. I was one of the lucky ones, I suppose, meant to live, meant to do the work I have been doing all these years around democracy and justice and equal opportunity, meant to write this letter to you today.

But, my child, I am also very human—unimaginably flawed —and I still carry around the profound scars of what I have endured, from experiences like these. Scars born of my childhood and youth. Scars born of my tumultuous adult years, of my years now in middle age, questioning, to be mad honest, how long I will be here on this earth, and what I can and should be for the rest of my life. Please do not get me wrong: I am clear who I am, what I do, but what I am talking about is my soul, my spirit, and the soul, the spirit, of America, of this planet. The past couple of years have been so very cruel, despite the joys of being married to my wife, despite the work I get to do. I have been steadfastly troubled by the violence, the hate, the fear, the ignorance, and the divisions that exist in our America. I have been steadfastly troubled by the absence of kindness, by the absence of compassion, by how foul and disrespectful so many people are toward each other, in public, on social media, like everywhere. I am scared, to be blunt, of bringing a Black child into this world, with s/he/ they having to deal with the same racism I and your mother encounter regularly, that we talk about every day. Racism is the sinister and deadly cancer in America. It is how your ancestral blood got here, through their capture and kidnap from Africa, through their enslavement; and our Native American blood, born to this soil, were the victims of the most grotesque genocide. Indeed, slavery was genocide as well, from the motherland, on board those human cargo ships, the bodies lost or tossed or that jumped themselves into the ocean, the bodies on those auction blocks, in New York where my wife and I live, in South Carolina where my mother and my entire family tree is rooted, through the madness of that slavery—spiritually, mentally, physically—that still haunts the American republic to this day. This is your birthright, my child, and it is also your curse, that you've got to come into this world, be you boy or girl, be you straight or queer, be you one gender identity or multiple gender identities or no gender identity at all; the ugly and mean-spirited reality is that you are Black, will be Black, and from the moment you begin to truly open your eyes and your pores and see America, and feel America, and hear America, and taste and smell America, it will become abundantly clear, soon enough, that you are hated by some because you are Black, and for no other reason. Some will say that I am lying, that I am exaggerating, but do not listen to them, my child, please listen to me, your father, please listen to your mother, please trust your own experiences, your own march through this land that is your land too, and know that no matter what the "they" that Black folks like to speak about say you are, who you can and cannot be, what you can and cannot do, you must ignore them, inside the third eye of your mind and your soul. Remind yourself, always, that you are a genius, that you are excellent, that you come from genius and excellence, that is in your DNA, from those queens and kings of Africa, through the Haitian Revolution and the Maroons of Jamaica, to the visionary leadership of Harriet Tubman, Sojourner Truth, and Ida B. Wells, to the majestic imagination of the Garvey Movement and the Harlem Renaissance and the Civil Rights Movement and Black Lives Matter, to all of our inventions and contributions to this experiment called America, to arguably the greatest gift our people has given this nation: our music. Yes, we are a massively wounded people because of what we have survived here, there is no question about that. But we are a beautiful and resilient people, too, and I want you to never forget that, that no matter what, no matter how many times you tumble or get knocked down, you must always get up, you must always keep it moving, forward. There is simply no other option, your very life demands that, and what your ancestors withstood demands that.

But, yes, and still, I found myself wanting to quit during various chapters of my journey, for this is how overwhelming life can be for us as Black folks in America, this is why I have dreaded, at times, the very thought of having a child. Indeed, my great friend Michael Cohen, a Jewish brother, says that racism in America is incurable, because it is in the very birthing of this country. Because I am a Black man in America who has witnessed the toxic nature of racism firsthand, I cannot say that I disagree with him. Mike is speaking truth. But I still have hope that America can change, that people like me, and people like you, my unborn child, can make America change. Hope is the energy that charges my body each day that I awake, that leads me to say each morning that I am thankful to be here. Hope is what my single mother had as she raised me from boyhood to manhood, in poverty, on welfare, with food stamps, in inhuman living environments, because she knew there was something better for me, for my life, if she could just hold on, if she could just keep herself, and me, alive. This is what I would do for you, have hope and give hope, that is my responsibility to you, my commitment to you. This is why you must not ever—**ever**—allow racism to stop you; you must not ever—**ever**—use racism as an excuse for why you cannot do all of what you've been put on this planet to do. Yes, you must challenge and question and move to eliminate racism at every turn. But you must also learn to navigate through it, around it, over it, under it, whatever you must do to live, yes, to survive, yes, to win, yes, while holding on, relentlessly, to as much of your sanity as you can. You will be in some spaces, for sure, where not only will White people not see you at all but, worse, they will see you for what they want you to be, not for all of who you are. You will be in some spaces, for sure, where some folks Black like you, because they have so obediently swallowed American racism, will similarly try to hurt or destroy you, will mock you, will dis you, will make you feel like you do not belong with them, either. In both instances you will get angry, you will become sad, you will be depressed, you will want to scream, spit profanities, and even perhaps hit or fight them, with your eyes, with your words, with your hands. I have done all of that and more. Some of it from my past I regret with great embarrassment, and some of it I know was the necessary and healthy release of a justifiable anger born of being Black and blue in America. Because few have been as loyal to the United States as us, serving the country, fighting in pretty much every single war, participating in every modern Summer Olympic Games, giving to America what America has never given to us: complete and unconditional love. It hurts to be invisible;

it hurts to be rejected; it hurts to be marginalized; it hurts to be treated as less than human.

And this is why I am terrified—twice over—if you happen to be born a girl, if you grow up identifying as a girl, as a woman. And the fact that you, like my wife and my mother, would have to deal with both racism and sexism your entire life. I think about this a lot because, as a man, I know what men do to women, what boys do to girls, and I think of how much my wife and I would have to do to prepare you, from a very early age, for the attempts to control and abuse and damage you, or destroy you, simply because you are a girl or a woman. The way Breonna Taylor and Sandra Bland were damaged, and destroyed. And I am also truly terrified, regardless of our best efforts, of your being touched by someone, beaten, raped, or murdered in cold blood because you are a girl, because you are a woman. Please know, if you happen to be born a girl, or transition to a girl or a woman during your lifetime, that you are the equal of any male, that you should never allow anyone to tell you what a girl or woman can and cannot do, that your mother and her mother and her grandmothers and my mother and my grandmother and my aunts are all extraordinary and strong and resourceful women, that that is what runs through your veins, and if you should ever wonder why the world is the way it is, also remember that no women have endured so much as Black women, and still do; that Gloria Steinem is right: that Black women truly are the original feminists, which means you can do anything, you can be anything, and you will.

And if you happen to identify as a boy, as a man, as a male, I want you to respect and honor women and girls as your equals—always. To never be—at any point in your life—what so many of us men and boys have been to women and girls: abusive, oppressive. I will teach you a different way to be a boy, a different way to be a man, one rooted in love, peace, nonviolence, and healthy ways of expressing yourself, not definitions that hurt you, as a male, or that will lead you to hurt other males, to hurt and have a reckless disregard for women and girls, as I was taught, as so many of us males have been socialized to be. Please know I will teach you these things from the very beginning, often, loudly, and I will also teach you to never put your hands on a woman or girl without permission, to never hurt or assault or violate a woman or girl physically, verbally, emotionally, spiritually; never to use destructive language to describe women and girls. I need you to hear me, clearly, if you happen to be a boy, a man. You must not make the same mistakes so many of us men and boys have made, generation to generation, culture to culture, across the entire universe. You must be different; you will be different.

And I need you to hear me, should you be a Black boy, to know that you will be viewed as dangerous, as an animal, as a monster, as a menace, by some, just because you are a Black male. My great fear, the great fear of my wife, would be getting a call one day, as my mother did many years back, that I was arrested, that you have been arrested. Our great fear would be your being killed, the way George Floyd was killed, the way Trayvon Martin was killed, the way Eric Garner or Michael Brown were killed, and many others, simply because they, you, are Black and male in America. This terror we would feel is unfair, is unreal, is the terror every Black parent has who has a male child or male children. That it will be their son next who is murdered in cold blood, because of who they are. These are the risks we take when we bring a child, children, into this world—

Finally, I pray that my wife and I can have you, will have you, despite what I have said here. That is because I love you very deeply, I need you, my wife needs you. I am not merely talking about the carrying forth of our family names and traditions, although those things do matter to us both. Nor am I talking about what we hope you will be, can be, although that too is important. I am talking about something far more special and far more urgent. We need you because we need love in all forms, and there is no greater gift, I believe, than love producing life, another life, and caring for that life, as we will do for you. Like our marriage, you would be a blessing to my wife, to me, to our lives together. Yes, the world can be a very cold and callous place, but in our home, you will know that you are loved, that you are appreciated, that your life truly is valuable, please know this, my child, please. And please learn fast, to smile, to laugh, to find humor even in the darkest corners, for that laughter will be the light guiding you from the bleakest tunnels to limitless highways. And please know that as we love and care for you, as you grow and come to understand both the material world and the spiritual world, that we will expect you to love and care for yourself—you must, even if no one else loves you except your mother and me; and we will expect for you to love and care for others, for there are few things more important, I believe, than to serve, than to give back.

For sure, I will want you to never forget that love is the greatest thing in creation, that you are love in the flesh, and we will not only love you unconditionally and unapologetically, but that we know when we send you out there, as a child, as an adult, as the unique human being you will come to be, it is with the hope and the promise that your life and your world will be much better than ours. And if some openly express hate and venom toward you, my child, you must respond with love always, despite the need to keep great distance from the haters. You must never become hate, or fear, or violence, or division, or ignorance. You must forever be the highest example of humanity, of what the world should be, not what the world is. This world is crazy, nasty, and—more times than not—despicably and embarrassingly soulless. Many do not possess an ounce of love, of compassion, of empathy. Many do not have any sort of spiritual or moral compass. But you must, my child, you must. For the sake of your own soul, for the sake of your own heart, for the sake of your own sanity, especially during the roughest times, and there will be many, I can guarantee that. Live, please, be free, be you, whoever you have been ordained to be. Be better than me, be better than your mother, be better than all who've come before you. That is my dream, that is my dream for you. And so it shall be....

Your father,
Kevin

BETWEEN RUSSELL SIMMONS AND THE WORLD AND OPRAH

Cause we're alone now
And I'm singing this song to you
–Donny Hathaway, "A Song for You"

TAKE 1

The godfather of hip-hop, Russell Simmons, sits at a table with two elderly White men on either side of him, holding court in the lobby of New York's Mercer Hotel, just days before Christmas. The Mercer is an epicenter of power and wealth, less a lobby than an exclusive living room for Simmons and other visitors. Once you push past the heavy black drapes that separate the outside world from this living room, there are art-deco shelves and tables filled with all kinds of books and high-end magazines; there are immaculately scrubbed white walls and comfortably elegant sofas; and there are young, chic, multicultural staffers rocking all-black gear while attending to the godfather of hip-hop and others milling about.

Simmons, with no security detail, is dining on a vegan burger, a salad, and a glass of water, totally at ease, his toothy grin engraved ear to ear, sporting his usual uniform of a New York Yankees fitted cap, a colorful button-up shirt, chiming prayer beads around his neck, blue jeans, and white-on-white Adidas sneakers. There is a sun-baked glow to Simmons' copper brown skin, the product of several years of daily yoga and meditation, and every kind of self-care activity at his well-manicured fingertips. Given what is hovering all around Russell Simmons' life this very moment, his Zen-like state is unbelievably jarring in its calmness.

A child of blue-and-white-collar Queens, New York, Simmons and his journey have been a testimony to the surge of hip-hop, the governing culture on the planet since the early 1980s. His vast and layered business interests have grown to include music, film, management, comedy, finance, television, books, fashion, media, technology, the visual arts, yoga, and poetry. There are few in pop culture who can say they have not been affected by Russell Simmons and his monumental reach.

I count myself among the nation of millions. When I was a teenager in the 1980s, I danced to—and worshipped—several of the hip-hop acts Simmons either guided via his firm Rush Management (like his younger brother Joseph's rap group, Run-DMC), or had on his now-historic record label, Def Jam (like LL Cool J, The Beastie Boys, and Public Enemy). In the 1990s, I was a senior writer at *Vibe* magazine, which Quincy Jones owned, and Simmons considered joining as a partner. When I was fired from the publication in 1996, it was Russell Simmons, while having a sidewalk lunch with the writer Nelson George at Greenwich Village's Time Cafe, who told me to get over the firing and "go franchise yourself."

In the late 1990s, I wrote cover stories on iconic figures like Lauryn Hill and Chris Rock for Simmons' *One World* magazine, although I never interacted with him directly. A year or two later, when I helped produce the very first exhibit on the history of hip-hop, with the Rock and Roll Hall of Fame and the Brooklyn Museum, it was Russell Simmons who I sat down with, along with the director of the Brooklyn Museum, to get his stamp of approval. And into the 2000s and 2010s I have become both a vegan and a yogi myself, due in no small part to the health-and-wellness preaching of individuals like Russell Simmons. But the only other time I can ever recall interviewing Russell Simmons was during the 1990s, as he was walking on a treadmill in his home in Manhattan. I have no clue who or what that interview was for, and my only recollection is him telling me I should try yoga.

Russell Simmons and I are not friends and have never been. But there has always been mad respect, and through the years, I certainly was in awe of him for curating a soundtrack and a culture that I grew up with, one that provided spaces of expression for me and Black and Brown boys like me from America's ghettos.

Because no Russell Simmons for hip-hop is like no Rosa Parks for the Civil Rights Movement, like no Frida Kahlo or Jean Michel-Basquiat for avant-garde painters, like no Michael Jordan for basketball or Nike, like no Beatles for innovative song-writing and sonic twists and shouts, like no Meryl Streep for method-inspired actors, like no Kardashians or Jenners for reality television and Instagram, and like no Oprah Winfrey for emotion-packed TV talk shows and teary-eyed confessional interviews.

His presence has been revolutionary and deeply transformative for multiple generations of hip-hop heads, a railway bridge between people and possibilities, making Simmons a very potent and very rich tastemaker in the process. As a matter of fact and keepin'-it-a-hundred mythmaking, Russell Simmons is the walking, breathing logo of manifesting something from nothing, of winning on his own terms—the very definitions of hip-hop.

As Simmons sits there with his vegan burger in the lobby of the Mercer, several people, mostly White, stop to pay their respects, to ask how he has been, to say it is good to see him, to shake or touch his hands. You can tell that these admirers have not encountered Simmons in a long while, or are surprised to see him, by their words, by their body language. That is because the godfather of hip-hop no longer lives in New York, or in America, but has resided, since February of 2018, in Bali, in Indonesia, in Southeast Asia, a nation-state that is a safe and extradition-free haven 9,000 miles away from the allegations of approximately 20 women who have accused Russell Simmons of, among other things, rape.

TAKE 2

The allegations began in late 2017, just as the #MeToo movement dramatically shifted conversations around sexism, around manhood, across America, across the universe. Hollywood mogul Harvey Weinstein went down first, fast and hard in October 2017, an avalanche of 80 allegations of rape, sexual harassment, and other sexually oppressive conduct. Mere weeks after Weinstein's fall from grace, the first wave of Russell Simmons' accusers came forth, as published in the *New York Times* in December 2017.

Say her name: Drew Dixon, a well-regarded music executive who says that in the mid-1990s, Simmons sexually harassed her during her employment at Def Jam Recordings, exposing his erect penis on several occasions, speaking explicitly to her on work calls, and eventually raping her at his Downtown Manhattan apartment. Close friends of Ms. Dixon have corroborated that she immediately told them about these allegations and left Def Jam with a "settlement" of $30,000—only $3,000 of which went to her directly, legal fees swallowing the rest of it.

Say her name: Sherri Hines, also known as pioneering female rapper Sherri Sher of Mercedes Ladies, the first all-women's rap group. In the early 1980s, Hines says, Simmons pinned her down on a couch in his sparsely furnished new offices and "violated" her sexually, after which she left in tears. Sheri Sher told close friends at the time, but never said anything publicly, for fear of being shunned in the music industry, and because she did not want to bring a Black man down. (Years later, in 2008, Ms. Hines wrote a novel based on the real lives of Mercedes Ladies, which depicts a businessman named "Ronald" who rapes a member of the women's rap group.)

Say her name: Sil Lai Abrams. A former model and currently a long-time domestic violence awareness activist, she says that she dated Simmons off and on for a few years, from the late 1980s through the early 1990s, but one night, while not in a relationship with him of any kind, he took advantage of the fact that she was drunk, and instead of having his driver take her home, she was brought to his residence. There, Abrams has alleged, Simmons raped her, as she laid on her stomach in his bed. It has been reported and confirmed that she was so distraught about the incident she immediately told close friends; the next day, Abrams says, she downed pills and wine in a suicide attempt.

These three women appear in the soon-to-be-released documentary film *On The Record* focusing on the allegations around Simmons, which recently premiered at the Sundance Film Festival to sold-out crowds. All told, there are numerous allegations and complaints against Russell Simmons: everything from rape to sexual harassment, according to various sources. Most of the allegations fall outside the statute of limitations for sex crimes, which is 21 years for New York State, where much of this is said to have occurred. While the pattern of allegations ranges from the 1980s to the 2010s, many episodes share a common thread: Simmons maneuvering women into compromising spaces like an office or an apartment, alone, where they have no escape route.

However, Simmons' supporters—ex-wife Kimora Lee Simmons, and about a dozen family members, and his past and present friends, colleagues, and business partners I spoke with—believe that some or all of these women are lying, that Russell Simmons would never be violent toward women.

"I have known Russell for over 25 years," Kimora wrote on Instagram in the aftermath of the allegations. "We were close friends, married, divorced, and have remained friends, co-parents and partners throughout it all. These allegations against him are nothing like the person I have known in all that time. I have known him to be a caring and supportive father and someone who has worked tirelessly to uplift disenfranchised communities."

I do not know which men are or are not rapists, sexual harassers, abusers, and batterers of women. What I do know is that my friend and fellow activist Tarana Burke coined the term "me too" in the first years of this twenty-first century as she was working with young Black and Latinx girls, and noticed that many of them, barely into their teens, had already been raped by a male figure—a man, a boy, or both. I did not know Tarana was doing this when she and I crossed paths doing relief work in the Deep South in the heartbreaking fog of Hurricane Katrina. By the time actress and singer Alyssa Milano encouraged legions of women to use #MeToo on social media on October 15, 2017, in response to the Weinstein revelations in *The New York Times* and *The New Yorker*, hundreds of thousands of women and girls had posted their own responses.

Yet, when Russell Simmons was accused, he employed a different hashtag: #NotMe. The backlash was swift from women, and men sympathetic to women, on Twitter, condemning Simmons for not taking sexual violence against women and girls seriously. What he does own, is his past womanizing: "I'm in this mess because of the amount of whoring I did," he says to me. "I am one thousand percent comfortable taking responsibility for what I have done, but I absolutely don't want to take responsibility for what I haven't done and that is that I'd never been violent, I've never been forceful, and [it was] never my intention to hurt anyone."

When #MeToo first exploded, there was no way to predict how many women would step forth to speak of being survivors, to name the men who had assaulted and or harassed them. Dozens upon dozens of men—executives, elected officials, journalists, names like Charlie Rose and Matt Lauer and Al Franken—have by now been accused of sexual transgression in one form or another. The #MeToo movement has forced a renewed interest in the cases of men like Roman Polanski and Woody Allen, and it landed Bill Cosby in jail. "This is going to go on for years," a famous actress friend told me at the start of the #MeToo movement. "Men being accused and held accountable." Perhaps this is why so many men are frightened, in entertainment, in music, in sports, in politics, in corporate America, everywhere—just like some White Americans were scared, during the Civil Rights Movement, as racism was being tested at every turn. Power forever panics under siege.

If we are to be honest, then we must acknowledge that America was founded not just on racism, but also on sexism. There has scarcely been a time from the beginning of this social experiment in "democracy" that our society has granted any women and girls value equal to men and boys—let alone to Black women and girls. The habitual and continuous rape of Black women by White male slave masters and White male overseers was not merely a passing feature of slavery, but a foundational weapon in its arsenal of dehumanizing tactics. (If you think otherwise, then peep the many colors and complexions of Black folks in this fair land and ask, How did that happen? Rape and sexual violence are tools of control, of oppression, of power gone insane.) In her film *NO! The Rape Documentary*, Aishah Shahidah Simmons asserts that Black male slaves consciously and subconsciously absorbed that mindset and began to view Black women and girls as little more than sexual toys, caretakers, or punching bags, just as the White male slave masters and White male overseers did. This was in spite of the fact that Black women and Black men were kidnapped from Africa together, put at the bottom of those slave ships together, worked in the fields and in the master's house together, celebrated emancipation together, fled white masks and hanging nooses together, and marched and got water-hosed and clubbed in the head together at civil rights protest after civil rights protest.

Evelyn and Daniel Simmons, Russell's parents, civil rights workers themselves, were together as they raised him—the middle child—and his two brothers, Danny Jr. and Joseph. But, according to Russell, "my parents fought all the time." He adds that his mother was fiercely independent, and "was the most nurturing person in my entire life. No one was more supportive of my dreams and my spirit like my mother, no one." Evelyn, a small woman in stature, worked for the Parks Department in Queens while Daniel Sr. was a history teacher, but her true passions were the arts, as she was both a painter and a poet (Danny Jr. would too become a painter and poet). College-educated and a dreamer like her son Russell, Evelyn would divorce her husband in the 1970s when Russell was a teenager, on the heels of Civil Rights, Vietnam, women's rights, and the flowering of major Black women writers like Ntozake Shange.

Russell does not know fully why his parents split, but coupled with the sexism and male privilege that all women have endured in this country, and the many movements, from suffrage to equal rights to #MeToo, that have pushed back on those hateful dynamics—imagine being a Black woman who not only has to deal with racism, but also sexism as well? This is why Gloria Steinem, a pioneer for equal rights for women for over 50 years, has said, loudly, that Black women in America are the original feminists. Because Ms. Steinem, and progressive White women like her, are clear that Black women have had to deal with an extraordinarily disproportionate amount of venom and violence because of their skin color and their gender.

Later, as hip-hop was being birthed by poor African-Americans, poor West Indians, and poor Latinx folks in The Bronx, it overlapped with the Civil Rights and Black Power Movements, neither of which would have happened without Black women front and center, but both of which witnessed men perpetrating sickening sexism and violence against Black women. I can't begin to articulate the number of Civil Rights-era Black women who have told me of the hate and brutality they endured fighting for a freedom that did not seem to comprise them. Over the past decade or so, I've been working on a biography of Tupac Shakur; Tupac's mother, Afeni Shakur, was one of the few women who fought back—and was vilified for it, her contributions minimized by those men who feared and loathed an outspoken woman.

We know there would be no hip-hop being officially born on a muggy August day in 1973 in the South Bronx if Cindy Campbell had not produced the very first event at which her brother Kool Herc deejayed—thereby pre-dating Russell Simmons' party-promoter hustle by half a decade. But hip-hop would certainly allow and encourage foul behavior toward women and girls, just like rock and roll before it. Giants named David Bowie, John Lennon, Mick Jagger, and members of Led Zeppelin have all been accused of an assortment of things, like sex with underage girls, like domestic violence, like rape. Hip-hop is merely the most recent pop culture phenomenon that is representing what has always been there: unapologetic sexism.

I did not know any of this as a boy who fell in love with hip-hop in the late 1970s. But even if you listen closely to that first major hip-hop hit, "Rapper's Delight," it is riddled with sexism and the objectification of women: *I can bust you out with my super sperm.* From childhood on, we learn much of what we know about manhood from music, from television, from movies, from sports, from male-centered spaces. In a call after he had returned to Bali, Russell Simmons speaks directly to these influences, saying "We grew up watching *The Mack*, I saw so much stuff, and so many people were living in a culture where they devalued women."

As a result, young males, generation to generation and culture to culture, were and are clueless about the male policing we do to each other "to prove our manhood," the sexist or homophobic words we toss at each other like verbal grenades, our brazen grabbing and touching of girls as if their bodies are our playgrounds. We do not know this is assault. We teach each other there is something wrong with you, sexually, as a boy, as a man, if you do not get sex, if you do not talk or brag about your sexual conquests, whether real or imagined. No, not all of us go on to rape and assault women once we became men, but rape culture lurks all about us, in language and in deed—

Add to this the fact that most of us learned little to nothing about the history and contributions of women and girls in school, in the mass media culture, in our religious or spiritual spaces; it is little surprise that many of us men and boys are entirely clueless about women and girls, about rape culture, about domestic violence, about gender discrimination. It becomes quite easy, with that enthusiastic ignorance, to blame women and girls for everything, to diss them, to never think twice about how they were treated, in my 'hoods in my hometown of Jersey City, right through my college years at Rutgers University.

For me it was not until my early twenties in July of 1991, while living with a girlfriend in Brooklyn, that my awakening occurred. How it happened was pitiful and toxic. During an argument, I didn't like a response from her—and pushed her, in a fit of rage, into the bathroom door. I cannot recall what the argument was about, but I do remember feeling a sense of powerlessness as my girlfriend challenged me, so I responded with violence. She bolted from the apartment barefoot, crying, and screaming. I stood trembling, mortified at what I had done. The pathetic thing would have been to say she caused me to do it, or that what she said happened did not actually happen. But I could not lie. My single mother had raised me to always tell the truth, and I thought often of her saying to me, to not be like my father. I was never clear what ma meant until that incident. *Do not become an abuser. Do not hurt women.*

I went for therapy, I consulted both women and men for guidance, I wrote an essay for *Essence* called "The Sexist in Me," apologizing for the incident and taking ownership for it. Years later I would apologize to my ex-girlfriend directly, and I have never put my hands on a woman in any un-welcomed manner since that day, but I would be lying if I said I have not said disrespectful and dishonorable things to women since, or that I have not been sexist. Because I have been; I am very clear about that, because all men are either sexist or are easily capable of being sexist instantly.

I struggled mightily, through the 1990s, through the heyday of my years at *Vibe*, as I participated in a culture that I knew was loaded with disgusting examples of manhood, such as Dr. Dre's savage beating of Dee Barnes, or rappers and crews punching hip-hop journalists who had given them negative reviews, or the bottomless survey of songs that called women every kind of name or curse word imaginable, or depicted every kind of sexual aggression, including rape, gang rape, and domestic violence. And just like rock and roll before it, sex, drugs, and liquor were as central to our culture as breathing. While this was happening, women in and around the music industry talked. They talked about rumored assaults and harassment by record executives, including

Russell Simmons. They talked about rappers with terrible sexual assault reputations. I just was not aware of much of this back then, but now I know, because several anonymous women have said this to me while writing this piece.

"There is not a music industry executive who did not sexually harass me. They used their power, their money, and their resources, and the things that they can offer; they trick us with the glitz and the glamour, and then they use their dicks to try to manipulate the situation. They come off as wanting to help you, but when you do not do what they say, they take everything away."

—Black woman (name withheld) who has worked in the entertainment industry for over two decades

This is the culture that spearheaded scenarios of rape and abuse and sexual harassment over and over again, in songs, at concerts, in hotels, in studios, while many of us turned our heads, or enabled it, or acted like it was not happening. Perhaps the most profound thing Tupac Shakur said to me after he was sent to prison for an alleged sexual assault incident with a young woman is that while he maintained his innocence, what he was guilty of was not thinking of her safety as he fell asleep, and as his friends pounced on her.

TAKE 3

Louis C.K. Brett Ratner. Dustin Hoffman. George H.W. Bush. Morgan Spurlock. Ben Affleck. Casey Affleck. James Franco. Aziz Ansari. Kevin Spacey. Robert DeNiro. Antonio Brown. Donald Trump.

These are some more names of famous men accused of one sexual misdeed or another. It is an unofficial but very much alive boys' club that thrives in the corporate and creative worlds, in academia and entertainment, in politics and media, and that has always been the case. There are long days, longer nights; the divisions between work and play are blurred, and if you suffer from an acute case of male privilege, then you believe that everything is yours to take, including women's bodies without permission.

This is why the #MeToo movement is necessary. This is why I never thought I would ever see anything like it when I confessed those years back to my own toxic manhood, or as I have worked with men and boys to re-define manhood throughout America and globally. Because there has been a staunch resistance to the truth, an allergic reaction, if you will, to viewing women as our equals. So we go out of our way to deny their voices, to silence them, to say they want money and fame, that they are haters, that they are trying to destroy men. This is what Russell Simmons says to me time and again during our many interviews. This is what Russell Simmons tells me time and again during our many interviews about the "files" he has on the women accusers.

This is what men do: Men re-assert manhood, if you are Harvey Weinstein or Russell Simmons, to highlight the good things you have done for others, for women, while ignoring the fact that doing great things for others does not preclude monstrous acts. Gangsters and drug dealers give away turkeys at Thanksgiving, toys at Christmas, while still damaging the communities they give back to. Because this is about power, and that is what the #MeToo movement is challenging—the unchecked and abusive power of men—just like the Civil Rights Movement and Black Lives Matter came to challenge the unchecked and abusive power of White supremacy.

I wonder about all of this as I am now the one sitting next to Russell Simmons with a vegan burger and fries and a glass of water in front of me. Russell casually reaches across me several times to grab a couple of French fries from my stash. I barely eat my burger, because I want to focus on every word he is saying. I have known him for half my life, but I realize I do not know Simmons, do not know what might have happened with him and women behind closed doors, as he keeps talking: "So anyway, then #MeToo happened, I lost my five charities. ... I mean I'm happy to live where I live. ... So I have a job and purpose, and I'm thrilled where I am. I don't need to 'come back' as a lot of men do ..."

I believe the women, Russell Simmons, I believe you raped them, I believe you sexually assaulted them, is what I want to say to him. Then he says "I don't want to be an advocate for men. I want to be an advocate for change. And I certainly want to be an advocate for the shift in consciousness. I think it's more inclusive and has women's energy and in our governance of our planet." I wonder if he realizes he is in fact an advocate for men only, for toxic manhood, every single time he says the women accusers are only doing this for fame and money, every single time he smears their characters, be it publicly or privately. I wonder if he realizes that you just cannot skip from women saying you raped or assaulted them to becoming a spiritual guru on Instagram, using that very spiritual practice as a way not to deal with the reality of damage that has been done to these women's lives.

FROM: Russell Simmons Silence Breakers and Survivors

We are more than victims of rape. We are Black women. We are mothers, daughters, sisters and friends insisting on our right to live and work free from sexual violence and abuse. We will not back down, and we will not be silenced. We are not afraid. When we raised our anguished voices to say, "No! Stop! Don't!" to Russell Simmons, he ignored us. Now, as we raise our voices in defiance of a culture that protects abusers and their enablers, he has tried to discredit us and to deny our truth. Russell Simmons and his enablers cannot intimidate us, bully us, or ignore us. Unyielding as a force, united in our resolve, we are Black women standing with survivors of all colors and we will not be silenced. #silenceisviolence #ustoo #lifteveryvoice #metoo

TAKE 4

When Simmons and I move to a sofa in the Mercer Hotel lobby, I question silently how many men actually know what "consent" means, as discussed in *NO! The Rape Documentary* and on many college campuses I have visited; that having sex with someone who is drunk or high is rape; that having sex with someone who is saying yes but is drunk or high is rape; that having sex with someone who is sober or high or drunk who says no or maybe or I don't know is rape; that someone who resists at first, then gives in, does not necessarily give consent, which equals rape. While the legal terms may vary state to state, morally and spiritually clear consent by a woman is something rarely considered by men of all ages who are later accused of rape.

I ask Russell Simmons what he thinks rape is, and his response is wildly unsettling, naively revealing, and I am both saddened and disgusted that a 62-year-old man with his wealth and power would say these words, referencing the polygraph tests he submitted to regarding the accusations: "I think a lot of people are guilty of a lot of things. What we used to call rape was violent. I took all my tests, one of my tests was, I've never been violent. I thought that was the answer. I said no, no. And then the detective thought—and he had been a detective and he had also worked for the FBI and he was one of the best polygraph people in the country. He explained to me what the definition of rape was."

"What is required now is a much deeper dive on the part of men. Men have to say, What is sexual abuse? What is harassment? What is domestic violence? What happened in my childhood that made me the kind of man who is capable of degrading a woman, demeaning a woman, beating a woman, hurting a woman, raping a woman? What happened in the culture? What was I taught in the culture? What did I learn? Why? Why am I doing this? What's driving me?"

—Eve Ensler, author of *The Apology* and playwright of *The Vagina Monologues*

The fact that he, like many men, still does not know what rape is, speaks volumes about what may have happened to the women who accuse Russell Simmons of that sexually violent act. My mind is a sagging load of emotions as he continues to talk, nervously, about the many allegations against him, about the "files" he has on his accusers that he insists will prove his innocence. I attempt to tune out some of the things he is saying about the women—about this one having a drug issue, about that one who says she was raped by her father, about her and her and her wanting money and fame—because this is a recurring thing with so many men: to never look inward at themselves, but to instead point fingers outward. This is how power operates inside the music industry, inside any and all spaces where men run things. If men are questioned or prodded, the knee-jerk reaction, time and again, is to say that the woman accusing is wrong, that it cannot possibly be men with the problem, but the women, for even daring to mention ugly and toxic behavior.

TAKE 5

On another early evening inside the Mercer Hotel, I am with Russell Simmons and two of his longtime associates. Kevin Leong is Russell's close friend and creative director and is helping him to reboot the Phat Farm clothing line. Hasaun

Muhammad is a confidant, friend, and associate. Both men have hung for about 25 years with Simmons, since the 1990s. We go riding in Simmons' super-sized black SUV, to a Uniqlo clothing store, to a cold-pressed juice bar, to a cryotherapy center where he and Leong get a quick treatment, to Simmons' favorite Indian restaurant. We conclude the night at The Roof, a boisterous sky lounge atop Ian Schrager's Public Hotel.

Everywhere we stop, people know Russell Simmons, ask him how he is doing, greet him with reverence. He appreciates the love, is thankful for it, as he sips on a glass of red wine at The Roof. But he is ready to go to bed. The man who has been partying and jet-setting for much of his adult life is more interested, the past several years, in rising early, to meditate, to practice yoga, to teach anyone who will join him, about wellness. Meanwhile, I feel as uncomfortable here as I did at the Mercer Hotel, wondering how someone accused of rape and assault and harassment by approximately 20 women could so effortlessly move from place to place, including this lounge, like there are no eyes whatsoever on him. Guilty or not, this is what extraordinary wealth and power, in the hands of a man, look like; no matter the storm, just keep going.

"I have many prayer beads that I use for meditation. They all include the image of the holy sound. In the beginning was vibration and that sound was is 'ohm.'"

—Russell Simmons, in a text message to me about his daily spiritual practice

I watch Simmons' regular Instagram Live chats where he leads dedicated followers in meditation, waxes poetic on the wonders of yoga and his vegan lifestyle, proclaims his love for truth, and seems to relish the chance to be his other self, the higher-consciousness self—"Uncle Rush"—who he says he has evolved into. I wonder how Simmons' soul juggles these two dangerously conflicting realities: the old Russell who is accused by a number of women of rape and sexual harassment; and the new Russell who proclaims he wants to be a part of the women's movement that will change the world, who is proud of the fact his two teenaged daughters with Kimora, Ming Lee Simmons and Aoki Lee Simmons, ages 19 and 17, know what consent is.

I have spoken with Russell many times over the past two months, in person, by cellphone, and I have read and watched and listened to virtually everything attached to these accusations about him. He mentions his daughters regularly, how proud he is that both are in college, what they mean to him. The last time I spoke with Russell was just a couple of weeks ago, one early morning, now that he is back in Bali after spending time both in New York City and St. Barts during the holiday season. He sounds very much like a man who is afraid and confused, his spirit broken in some ways because of the documentary film that is coming. Once more, he says the words "I am sorry"—this is in relation to being "insensitive" to one of the accusers, Jenny Lumet—but, still, he maintains he never raped anyone. "You know what Ashley Judd told me?" he says. "I was really upset. I called her because I know she's one of the leaders of the movement. I said, 'This is crazy. I would never harm anybody.' She said, 'Revolution is bloody.'"

"I'm interested in not having my kids think I'm a rapist," he says. Every time he references his daughters, I think back to something I said a year ago to a group of students at James Madison University in Virginia, where I was a visiting professor: that men need to understand that all women and girls are our daughters, mothers, sisters, aunts, grandmothers, nieces. Afterwards, a young woman came up to me and corrected me, rightfully. "It should not matter if men have daughters or see any women as someone close to them," she said. "We should not have to say that all women are this or that. Women and girls should be honored and respected just because we are human beings."

The young woman was correct, is correct: Do men value women and girls as human beings, or not? And it is not enough to listen to women when they make statements, when they say they have been raped or hurt in some way. Sexism will not end until men are actively engaged in helping to make it end. That is not to say that men cannot grow, change, or at least begin to re-think and re-define manhood. I think of the crisis that unfolded between Beyoncé and JAY-Z when her video album *Lemonade* dropped, an undisguised and public challenge from Bey to JAY to do the right thing, due to his cheating and lack of respect for her. Equally important was JAY's response album, *4:44*. Perhaps with the exception of the evolution of John Lennon from violently abusive boy-band member to grown man proclaiming his love and reverence for Yoko Ono, we've rarely seen a male public figure with such a massive platform openly apologize the way JAY did. Between Russell Simmons and the world and Oprah, this is what the women I know, including my mother in her 76 years of life, have been looking for. A humble, genuine apology, an effort to heal, to grow up—to be, as Lizzo's words are remixed, great—especially when we men need to be great.

* * *

This, I believe, is what Oprah Winfrey was trying to say as early as 1991, when she featured the rapper Ice-T on an episode of her talk show. It was a combative segment, when guests and audience members went back and forth, talking over and through each other, dissing each other; you can tell by Oprah's body language and frozen facial expressions that she either hated or strongly disliked hip-hop. I think it no coincidence that through the years hardly any rappers have ever been in her orbit, except for the transcendently wealthy and successful ones, like JAY-Z. In one infamous episode, Oprah welcomed the cast of the film *Crash*, then used it as an opportunity to lambast the rapper Ludacris about his lyrics. And there has been a running beef between her and rapper and actor 50 Cent. All of which is why many in the Black and hip-hop communities called foul when Oprah Winfrey announced that she and Apple TV+ were jumping aboard Amy Ziering's and Kirby Dick's *On The Record* documentary featuring at least three of Simmons' accusers. In a society where Black people in general have been historically dissed just for being Black, it is easy to understand why we are hyper-sensitive to any critiques of, say, Michael Jackson, or Russell Simmons, why we are quick to say What about the White men? as if we Black men should get a pass, just because we are Black, for equally bad behavior.

The way the story goes, Oprah was blown away by a screening of the documentary and instantly jumped on board as executive producer, using her Apple TV+ partnership to leverage distribution. The documentary's credibility was already high—Ziering and Dick are Oscar-nominated filmmakers—but Oprah's involvement devastated Simmons, who had considered her a friend. Black people, seemingly spurred from a post by 50 Cent on Instagram, accused the billionaire media mogul of only going after Black men. A social media pile-on followed, with commenters on Instagram and elsewhere questioning Oprah's allegiance to the Black race, calling her an "Uncle Tom," and even suggesting she be canceled permanently.

Dearest OPRAH,you have been a shining light to my family and my community. Contributing so much to my life that I couldn't list a fraction of it in this blog. I have given you the gift of meditation and the groundbreaking book "THE POWER OF NOW" we bonded to say the least. This is why it's so troubling that you choose me to single out in your recent documentry. I have already admitted to being a playboy more (appropriately titled today "womanizer") sleeping with and putting myself in more compromising situations than almost any man I know. Not 8 or 14 thousand like Warren Beatty or Wilt Chamberlain, but still an embarrassing number. So many that some could reinterpret or reimagine a different recollection of the same experiences. Please note that ur producers said that this upcoming doc was to focus ONLY on 3 hand chosen women. I have refused to get in the mud with any accusers, but let's acknowledge what i have shared. I have taken and passed nine 3-hour lie detector tests (taken for my daughters), that these stories have been passed on by CNN, NBC, BUZZFEED, NY POST, NY MAG, AND OTHERS. Now that you have reviewed the facts and you SHOULD have learned what I know; that these stories are UNUSABLE and that "hurt people hurt people". Today I received a call from an old girlfriend from the early 1980s which means that they are using my words/evidence against me and their COMMITMENT/ (all of the claims are 25 to 40 years old) It is impossible to prove what happened 40 years ago, but in my case proof exists of what didn't happen, mostly signed letters from their own parents, siblings, roommates, band members, interns, and in the case of 2 of your 3 accusers,their own words in their books. Shocking how many people have misused this important powerful revolution for relevance and money. Maybe you should name your documentary "FLAVOR OF LOVE"!? In closing, I am guilty of exploiting, supporting, and making the soundtrack for a grossly unequal society, but i have never been violent or forced myself on anyone. Still I am here to help support a necessary shift in power and consciousness. Let us get to work on uplifting humanity and put this moment and old narrative behind us

—Russell Simmons, in an Instagram post

I talked with Simmons practically every single day for a month, and practically every single day he mentioned that he and Oprah had spoken, both before and after this Instagram post to her. She was trying to convince Simmons to do an interview with her, and he was trying to convince Oprah to drop out of the film as executive producer, to stop the film completely. She was doing her due diligence by reaching out to the "witnesses" Russell insisted could prove his innocence, and he was doing his due diligence by sending Oprah his "files" on the women accusers, which he insisted, to her, to me, to any who would listen, poked huge holes in their allegations.

Part of this dance between Simmons and Oprah, I believe, stems from Oprah's controversial interview with Michael Jackson's accusers around the time of HBO's *Leaving Neverland*. Many took to social media and suggested Oprah had crossed the line in supporting White people who were badly shredding the legacy of Michael Jackson without sufficient facts. And there has been a perception for many years that Oprah—the most powerful and influential woman on the planet outside of Hillary Clinton and Michelle Obama—goes out of her way to cater to White people, while not extending the same treatment to Black people. The facts make that perception a bit shaky: Be it Oprah's generous donations to historically Black colleges, her building of a major girls educational and art institution in South Africa, her many private donations to help Black folks of all kinds, and her complete and total embrace of the work of Black writers like Toni Morrison and Maya Angelou and Ta-Nehisi Coates, it is simply a lie that Oprah Winfrey does nothing for Black people in America or anywhere else.

"The woman is an independent entity. She is one of the few that we have, which means that she has not been bowing to White corporate interests for a long time because she owns her own shit. So what Uncle Tom?"

—Joan Morgan, author of *When Chickenheads Come Home to Roost: My Life as A Hip-Hop Feminist*

But what may be correct is her dislike of hip-hop, the way it has depicted women from the very beginning, and how so few of us in hip-hop culture or the hip-hop industry have been held accountable for our words and deeds, let alone taking responsibility ourselves. We must not forget that Oprah herself was sexually assaulted as a girl, that she herself is a survivor—so part of this work for Oprah, I am sure, is intensely personal. And just because Oprah is a billionaire with power and influence does not mean that she herself still does not carry around the scars, the traumas, of being that young Black girl who was abused, ridiculed, shamed, right into her early adult years. Surely, Oprah's story is not that different from many Black women, including my mother's. Oprah, my mother, an endless line of Black women, generation to generation, have not only had to deal with racism, just like Black men, but also have had to suppress, in the past and in the present, over and over, any conversations about sexism or gender oppression, often out of faithfulness to Black men, because of the ever-looming threat of White supremacy, and even if certain Black men are not loyal to them. But at what cost to Black women's bodies, souls, mental health? My grandmother loved my grandfather fiercely to the day he died, but he hit her when he felt like it, cursed her out when he felt like it, and expected her to have babies and raise the children and take care of him, because he, a Black man, had so few places to hold power in this White-male-dominated universe, other than over his wife. At home, in sports, in entertainment, in hip-hop, we get to be the kings of the world, while not realizing that our very definitions of manhood are eerily the same as those of White men in power—a bootleg definition of White manhood, yes, that is rooted in a reckless disregard for people.

Because of the marriage of racism and sexism, Black women truly are the mules of the world, as Zora Neale Hurston wrote in her classic and timeless novel *Their Eyes Were Watching God;* and Black women have never been regarded in the same breath as White women, and that would emphatically include this era of #MeToo. If most of Russell Simmons' accusers were White women, some believe, he would have been charged with crimes already, and more than likely on his way to prison, like Bill Cosby.

It was known throughout the music industry for two decades—two decades—that R. Kelly was a serial abuser of Black females, particularly young Black girls, but it was dismissed, ignored, joked about, and enabled, because they were Black. Tarana Burke was only acknowledged as the true creator of the #MeToo movement when Black women took to social media in October of 2017 and pushed back on the notion that Alyssa Milano had coined the phrase. Black women are not, and have never been, valued in the way White women are—in America, or on this planet. Racism has demanded that White women, from slavery forward, represent the standards of beauty, honor, and dignity, that they be the lens through which Black women and other women are viewed. So, yes, Tarana Burke is now widely hailed as the creator of #MeToo, but White women's stories are still elevated in a way that Black women's stories are not. Perhaps this is what brought Oprah Winfrey to this film about Russell Simmons and the Black women who are accusing him: In hearing the stories of women like Drew Dixon and Sherri Sher and Sil Lai Abrams, Oprah was also bearing witness to herself on that screen.

But Black men damaged by both racism and sexism will not grasp this, will instantly become reactionary and defensive, will say that Black women are attacking the Black man, that these Black women are traitors to Black men, to the Black race. This is partially because even in this era of #MeToo, the optics suggest that while Black males like R. Kelly and Bill Cosby are in jail or will wind up in jail, White males accused of comparable crimes and misdeeds will not be. In other words, history and current scenarios paint the picture of Black males as the poster children, time and again, for male bad behavior, even if accused White men have lost careers too. Because we Black males are treated far harsher, condemned far harsher, punished far more severely, in life, and even in death, per Michael Jackson, per Kobe Bryant, while White males who have been accused of similar toxic behavior are either given a pass, or allowed to bounce back, in some form, eventually, in life, in death. That is our perception, what is in our gut, as Black men. Because the image of the Black male as predator, as violent criminal or violent abuser, and so on, is as old as racism itself, and is a very blatant creation of racism.

Are there Black males who truly are rapists, abusers, batterers, child molesters, serial adulterers, murderers, menaces to society? Without question. But the vicious racism of our world makes it nearly impossible for the average Black male to even grapple with sexism, sadly, tragically, and Black women suffer as a result, because "intersectionality" is as foreign to some Black males, and other men of other cultures, as the word sexism. Meanwhile, as I write this piece, the Harvey Weinstein trial has been unfolding in New York, with additional charges pending in Los Angeles; yet, his insurance company, not him, is paying off a wave of his accusers. Weinstein does his best to solicit sympathy by entering court daily with a walker, appearing to be in feeble health. If Weinstein actually winds up spending a single day in jail, it would come as an astonishment to Black folks of all genders—because even within the era of #MeToo, White male privilege remains alive and well.

"The truth is … truth that he's using power? Absolutely, everywhere. All the time. Did he punish people for not agreeing, not doing it? I'm sure. Some people could've got a part if they had done it. And, some people got a part even if they didn't do it. Right? A lot of that. So, did people sleep their way into parts other people should've got? Yeah, probably. Right? And, did people who don't, who couldn't be any good in the movies get the part? Probably not and probably people are mad because they didn't get what they wanted. I don't know, man. I don't want to defend Harvey Weinstein. Fuck him."

–Russell Simmons

But it is not just about Harvey Weinstein and White male privilege, it is about male privilege period, including, as Russell Simmons displays above, the privilege of doubting the testimonies of victims, even in the case of someone like a Harvey Weinstein. In other words, either you are a serial rapist and serial abuser, or you are not. Either you stand on the side of women who've come forth, and listen and hear them, or you become an accomplice to the oppression of women. There are no gray areas here. Because Russell Simmons, like Harvey Weinstein, is using the male playbook of men who want to duck or dodge truth while holding firmly to toxic manhood. Thus, what men who refuse to be held accountable are guilty of, at the least, is unapologetic sexism in how they respond to accusations, bullying and intimidating women who have accused them, and even going so far as to harass their associates or family members. So in commenting on Weinstein, is Simmons also commenting on himself?

TAKE 6

People are anxious, nervous, scared. Or so it seems. Over the two months that I have been researching and writing this article, there have been a number of individuals who have refused to talk on the record, or who have completely ignored me, including Oprah Winfrey's office (no reply); the office of the documentary producers Amy Ziering and Kirby Dick (no reply); music industry insiders who know either Russell Simmons or his accusers or both (no one wanted to speak on the record); even the New York Police Department. When I reached out to the person who was the lead detective for the many allegations of rape and sexual violence against Russell Simmons here in New York City, the detective, a White man, responded via a social media platform that he had no comment. I sent another NYPD spokesperson—a Black woman —a LinkedIn message about the allegations, and she replied with an email for me to use, and a number for me to call, to make sure they received my email. When I called the number to see if my email had been received, I was told they had no idea what I was talking about, to call back later, to talk with the Black woman who had sent me their way in the first place. And, finally, the lead woman accuser in the film, Drew Dixon, via her publicist, opted not to be interviewed by me for this piece, either, after agreeing to do so in person, twice, which dejected me. In more than 30 years as a journalist, I have never worked on any article where so many people either ignored my outreach, or asked to be off the record, or first said yes to an interview then declined.

TAKE 7

"I have decided that I will no longer be executive
producer on The Untitled Kirby Dick and Amy Ziering
Documentary, and it will not air on Apple TV+. First and
foremost, I want it to be known that I unequivocally
believe and support the women. Their stories deserve to be
told and heard. In my opinion, there is more work to
be done on the film to illuminate the full scope of what the
victims endured, and it has become clear that the filmmakers
and I are not aligned in that creative vision."

–Oprah Winfrey, in a statement

I was told, privately and by a very reliable source close to the
situation, that the Black women in the then-untitled
documentary, as well as other Black women who had accused
Simmons of various sexual transgressions, felt hurt, confused,
scared, and abandoned by Oprah's decision to pull out of the
film. This source said it struck them as bizarre that the same
Oprah Winfrey who raved about the documentary and signed
on instantly is the same Oprah Winfrey who now says she and
the producers "are not aligned in that creative vision." In the
meantime, the producers went on record in the *Los Angeles
Times* after Oprah's statement, saying they had no indication

whatsoever that she had any issues with the documentary. Then there is the matter of some women, in the film, not being told fully the nature of the film:

"It's news to me that this is a film about Russell Simmons. It was certainly not presented that way to me when I interviewed for it. The producers, what Amy and Kirby said, was that they really wanted to do an exploration of hip-hop culture in this moment of #MeToo, that they were very honest that they are examining the accusations that were brought about by Drew Dixon. I know Drew. So I didn't have any problem. But the fact that this is now like the Russell Simmons film is news to me. I'll be really honest about that, because that's not the way it was presented."

–Joan Morgan

Again, Russell Simmons was hoping, in his almost daily calls or texts with Oprah Winfrey, that she would look at his files, call his witnesses, and rethink her participation in the film. "America trusts her, she's very important," he tells me. "A misstep on her part could really hurt the women's movement. And they need her, we need her for that. We need her to lead the women's movement and add some compassion and some understanding to it. We can't afford for her to be seen as just another finger pointer, a man basher."

But in reality, it is not the place of Russell Simmons or any man to say what a woman should or should not do with her voice, her work, her platform. Nor is it our place as men to say how women should respond to allegations of sexual violence against women by men. Nor do we know if the very personal taunts from 50 Cent and others across social media got to Oprah about her race loyalties. What we do know, per her statement, is that she had creative differences with the producers, but still believes the women. While it is true Russell Simmons took nine lie detector tests, and passed them all, we also know that the way questions are asked during a lie detector test can affect the results, and that has been scientifically proven.

And what I do know is if several women have said the same man has raped or abused or sexually harassed them, over the course of years, then there is truth somewhere in those many women's stories, because I do not believe that multiple women would be lying about the same man. What I do know for sure is that 1 out of 3 women and girls on the planet will be the survivors of some form of sexual violence in their lifetimes—over one billion women and girls. What I do know is that whenever any powerful man, before and during the #MeToo era, has been accused of raping or otherwise injuring a woman or girl, the pattern is always the same: deny, question, and denigrate the character of the accuser; claim, as a man, to be the victim. What I do know is that countless women routinely endure unwanted touching, unwanted comments, unequal pay for equal work, belittlement of their contributions and ideas, attacks on their self-worth, vicious stereotypes, low expectations, ridiculously high standards for certain positions that are not required of men, and a general disregard for their welfare and their safety.

"We actually don't rape ourselves. This has been an issue about men, and I think we can call out men for eternity, but unless men actually change, we're going to be here for as long as the climate crisis allows us to be."

–Eve Ensler

The justifiable rage of many women in this era of #MeToo is understandable, just as my mother's lifelong rage toward my now-dead father has been. But is it enough to simply cancel men who engage in any form of sexual violence or harassment, to exile them so they simply disappear? Is "cancel culture" an answer to ending sexism? I do not think so: People are gone, but the system of sexism remains in place for the next rapist, the next abuser, the next harasser, to come along.

Imagine if the Civil Rights Movement, led by figures like Ella Baker, Fannie Lou Hamer, and Dr. King, among many others, simply canceled White Americans for their physically and emotionally violent racism toward Black people from 1619 onward. Imagine if there had been no love, no nonviolent protest, no forgiveness, no attempts whatsoever to heal the very wicked disease of racism?

Black people and other people of color then and now have every right to be angry at White America, from the horrors of slavery, to lynching during segregation, to hideous racial murders like that of Sandra Bland and Trayvon Martin in this century. We have done nothing to deserve this sort of treatment, nonstop, simply because we are Black, just like women have done nothing to deserve rape and harassment and groping and name-calling and more, nonstop, simply because they are women.

Yet I also think about a conference I attended a few months ago in San Francisco, a Women's Funding Network event that featured 400 participants from across the world. I was invited as a male ally, a male accomplice, to speak about what should be next, for men and boys, during this era of #MeToo. Less important than what I said is what was said to me by many of the women who were trying to figure out what to do in relation to husbands, fathers, grandfathers, brothers, and perhaps most critically, their sons. Just like we must stop expecting Black people and other people of color in America to do the heavy lifting of ending racism, we as men cannot expect women alone to do the heavy lifting of ending sexism and sexist violence.

Very few women I have ever met and talked with and listened to, who have been hurt in some way by men, have ever said to me very directly "I want revenge," let alone "I want money" or "I want to be famous" or anything else that powerful men so love to attribute to them. Why would any woman willingly subject herself to public scorn and ridicule, as has happened time and again—from Anita Hill to Desiree Washington to the accusers of Harvey Weinstein—for saying, publicly, a man has raped or abused or harassed them? What they want, I have heard over and over, is justice.

Are there false accusations? Without question. Do I know men who have been accused of foul things that they have not done? Without question. Are men and boys I encounter in my work as an activist and public speaker frightened about what they can and cannot do, what they can and cannot say? Yes, I have heard this, over and over, always in confidence, because of social media's power to destroy people with one click, because these men and boys are afraid that they will be accused of something, just because they are men and boys. I have had grown men say to me they now go out of their way not to even look women in the eyes, at work, on elevators, anywhere, for fear of one allegation or another; that they will no longer argue or debate with a woman for fear of being accused of being disrespectful, abusive, or a typically sexist man. I also have found myself staring down at the floor when it is just a woman and I am on an elevator, or some other tight space, knowing I am not that kind of man to harass anyone, but terrified that someone will say it anyway. But we know fear and avoidance are not the solution, are not a solution.

My hope is that men and boys can get to a space of redemption and reconciliation and love and anti-sexist actions as ways to combat and end sexism—as Dr. King and Nelson Mandela both once said about racism—where men and boys can be trained and re-trained on what is possible with a healthy kind of manhood that uplifts, not hurts, and where men and boys can have honest and vulnerable conversations about who we are, how we got here, and where we can go now that #MeToo has shifted everything, forever.

TAKE 8

"So, no one feels like they owe anybody silence anymore. And for the Black community in particular who have constantly trafficked in that, making women make the choice between the advancement of the race ... or the battle against racism over the battle against patriarchy, as if that is secondary. ... If Black men win, then they take care of the community. We've never seen that happen. Between that never happening and this cultural zeitgeist of accountability, it's a real moment for people who have never had to question or think that their behavior was ever going to be called into question or that there would be ramifications about it."

–Joan Morgan

I do not know what is going to happen to Russell Simmons: if there will be more accusations, if he will ever be charged, if he will ever spend a day in jail. Men like Russell Simmons and Bikram Choudhury and Roman Polanski have left the scenes of their alleged crimes, and live elsewhere, away from America where the accusations occurred. To be seen as fleeing is not a good look for men, for women, for humanity; meanwhile, these men continue to do their work, they continue to make money in some way, as Simmons is doing with new business ventures in Asia; and they continue to deny they ever did anything wrong, and people around them and people who admire or worship them, continue to never ask the tough questions of them, of ourselves: Why do so many of us ignore or silence the voices of women when they say they have been hurt in some way? Why do we have such a reckless disregard for the lives and sanity of women and girls, for half the world's population?

You do not have to be a rapist or a batterer or a harasser to be part of the problem. Saying nothing, or acting like the problem does not exist, or blindly blaming the women, makes you just as guilty. I also do not know if a Russell Simmons can be one of the leaders of a hypothetical men's movement, to help change manhood once and for all, given the huge gaps between what the women accusers are saying and what he is willing to take ownership for. But I do know Oprah Winfrey was right in a text she sent to him, and that Simmons read to me slowly: that it would be "monumental" if someone with his global platform were to speak freely and honestly about everything–

But is that remotely possible, given how revealing and convincing the women are in the film *On The Record*, and given how damaging that documentary is for Simmons and his claims of total innocence? It is an excellent case study: It is poetically made, handcrafted like the patched-up quilts ancient Black grandmothers fingered together with their souls –inside those patches, stories like those of Drew Dixon, Sil Lai Abrams, and Sheri Sher overlapping, women who refuse to allow men to damage them ever again, just like my mother and countless other mothers will not, ever again. HBO has purchased *On The Record* post-Sundance, and you will have to decide for yourself what all this is, was, and could be. But if you watch this film the way I watched it, you wonder how and why Oprah Winfrey would walk away, searching for the real reason, and how and why she could separate herself from these Black women and this film, which is like separating herself from herself. Only Oprah knows the whole truth, and perhaps Russell Simmons, godfather of hip-hop, does too—

And, honestly, this has been the most difficult piece I have ever written in my life. My emotions are bleeding, I have had painfully sleepless nights, as this story has dragged on, and on, and on. As a Black man, I do not ever want to see another Black man go down in a world already seemingly designed for us to fall. But by the same token I do not want to see Black women—or any women of any background—sacrificed just to spare a Black man—or any man of any background—accused of wrongdoing. This hurts me from all sides, every part of it. I have been a combination of angry and sad, because of the very real and very vivid stories of the many women who've come forth, and because Russell Simmons had been a hero of mine, a hero for many of us boys in the 'hood. When he made it, we made it. When he dreamed big, we dreamed big. He was us and we were him. I could not have imagined these kinds of allegations against him when I first saw him in person at some New York City event in the early 1990s, when I just stared, because there he was, and I was too timid to greet him. I just stared, hoping whatever magic he had rubbed off on me, a poor boy from the ghetto. Nor could I have imagined, all these years later, that he would be a fallen hero, desperately trying to prove his innocence, thanking me just for listening to him, me, the writer who had found his voice, long ago, because of the culture—our culture—Russell Simmons helped to bring to the entire world.

But I believe the women, Russell Simmons, I believe you raped them, I believe you sexually assaulted them ...

So, yes, it would be "monumental" if Russell Simmons were to come forth in the fearless way he came forth with hip-hop. Yes, if he were to encourage other men and boys to do the same. Russell Simmons is still a hero and a godfather of hip-hop to many, but even heroes and godfathers can be very fragile and very afraid and very much in need of healing, too. Russell said many times in our conversations that "hurt people hurt other people," and I now wonder if he meant every single one of us, including himself, particularly because of one phone call from Bali where he struggled mightily to talk about his mother, about his father, about their relationship, and he could not recall which of them died first. This man with all he has done professionally and all he is dealing with now personally, in that instance, was reduced back to the young boy he once was. Hurt people hurt other people—So, alas, what I do know is that real change must occur, and occur very soon, with Russell Simmons, with all of us men, with all of humanity, because women of every race and culture and creed have spoken, are speaking, and they will never be silent again.

A LETTER TO MY 9-YEAR-OLD FRIEND DURING THE CORONAVIRUS PANDEMIC

Dear Lexington:

I am scared, too, I have been crying, too, I have nightmares, too—these are the words I should have said to you yesterday on the phone, but did not, so I say them today. Your mother shared with me what you have been going through during the course of this coronavirus pandemic. You are not alone. Once upon a time I was a nine-year-old child, and many things shook my soul, interrupted my sleep, made me afraid of the dark, made me hold tight to my single mother, just as you hold tight to your single mother. There were many things I did not understand, back then, but I remember hearing words like "Vietnam" and "Watergate" and "recession" a lot, and I thought those words were coming to get me. I remember, like you, being profoundly sad, wanting to scream, become invisible, and feeling mightily stuck in my fear and pain.

But I need you to know this is part of the journey. Nothing could have prepared me for the many pandemics of my life: the ugly poverty, the racism, violence everywhere, those dreadful periods of loneliness of being a highly sensitive only child, just like you are a highly sensitive only child. Kids would mock or dis me, like kids mock or dis you. Kids would say something is wrong with me, as kids have said something is wrong with you. Kids would refuse to engage or play with me outside, as kids have refused to engage or play with you online during this time of human isolation. I am here to say that you are not the problem, that you are who I wish I could have been when I was nine-years-old: a boy very much in touch with his feelings, because you are a genius and a gift to your mother, to me, to this entire world.

But I will not lie to you. I am worried every day by what has happened to our beloved New York City, to our country, to our planet, because of this global pandemic. I personally know people who have died, including friends, people I have worked with or admired, and one of my cousins. Or I am just one degree separated from someone who was taken down by COVID-19, someone's mother or father or some other relative. Or I know people who are nurses, doctors, employees in supermarkets and restaurants, or other frontline workers, sacrificing themselves, some because they have no other choice financially. My heart hurts badly thinking about these many people and their families.

I live this hurt daily, as you do, even if it is something as simple as checking mail, or going for a quick walk, or shopping at the grocery store. Will my mask and gloves really protect me, should I be outside? I have gone days not wanting to leave home, just like you have not wanted to leave home. I am terrified, as a human being, as a Black person, of catching the virus, because of the scary statistics. And because I am both an activist and a journalist, I absorb news updates about the coronavirus regularly which, I am sure, has contributed to the worst nightmares I have ever had. Honestly, I have not thought of dying so much since I was a little boy hearing stories from my mother about kinfolks who had died, or the sermons in our church, which always seemed to be a lesson about the small gap between life and death.

So I understand you, I know what you are feeling, what you are carrying, because I am you. I am here to tell you that you can call me any time, to talk, to yell, to be silent and just breathe, to cry, and I will cry with you. I am here to tell you not to become like some in this moment where hate is as necessary to them as their heartbeats. I am here to tell you to never become mean or cold-hearted or a bully, in spite of what you might see or hear all around you.

And I am here to tell you that I do not know what is going to happen to our city, to our country, to our world, but what gives me hope is that I am seeing the best of us as Americans, as human beings, coming together, helping each other, feeding each other, caring for each other. It reminds me so much of what I witnessed after September 11th here in New York; it reminds me so much of what I experienced for a year doing relief work back and forth in the American South after Hurricane Katrina.

What I am saying is that we cannot allow this to defeat or destroy us. No, everything will not be completely fine right away. There will be more deaths, more tears, more depression, this I know. There will be more false starts and false promises from some of our leaders, this I know.

But for those of us who will survive this, like you, like me, we must commit everything we can, to do better, to be better, to love and honor every human being, to love and honor our earth, to be the consistent kindness and healing and forgiveness and love we need to see, for the rest of our lives.

Your friend,
Kevin

we them people

dream on
dreamer
the way Alvin Ailey
and Maya Angelou
and George Floyd
and Breonna Taylor
dreamed of
southern-baked
pilgrims
dancing and
slow marching
their sorrows
down the yellow
brick roads
of
second-line members
humming from

the heels of their dirt-kissed feet:
i wanna be ready/to put on my long white robe....
we are survivors
we are survivors
we are survivors
of people
who were free
and became slaves
of people
who were slaves
and became free
we know why the caged bird sings
we know what a redemption song brings
we them people
we the people
we are those people
who shall never forget
our ancestors all up in us as we sleep
our grandmother all up in us as we weep
because we are
native american
black irish welsh french german polish italian
jewish puerto rican mexican greek russian
dominican chinese japanese vietnamese
filipino korean arab middle eastern
we are biracial and we are multicultural

we are bicentennial and we are new millennial

we are essential and we are frontline

we are everyday people and we are people everyday

we are #metoo we are #metoo we are #metoo

we are muslim christian hebrew too

we are bible torah koran atheist agnostic truer than true

we are rabbis and imams and preachers and yoruba priests

tap-dancing with buddhists and hindus and rastafarians

as the Nicholas Brothers

jump and jive and split the earth in half

while Chloe and Maud Arnold

them syncopated ladies

twist and shout and stomp and trump

hate

again—

again—

again—

yeah

still we rise still we surprise

like we got Judith Jamison's crying solo in our eyes

every hello ain't alone every good-bye ain't gone

we are every tongue every nose every skin every color every

face mask

we are mattered lives paint it black

we are mattered lives paint it black

we are mattered lives paint it black

we are every tattoo every piercing every drop of blood every
global flood
we are straight queer trans non-gender conforming
we are she/he/they
we are disabled abled poor rich
big people little people in between people
we are protesters pepper-sprayed with knees on our necks
we are protesters pepper-sprayed with knees on our necks
we are protesters pepper-sprayed with knees on our necks
we them people
we the people
we are those people
who will survive
these times
because we done
survived
those times
where pandemics were
trail of tears and lynchings and holocausts
where pandemics were
no hope and no vote and no freedom spoke
we them people
we the people
we are those people
while our planet gently weeps
we bob and bop

like hip-hop
across the tender bones
of those tear-stained photographs
to hand to
this generation
the next generation
those revelations
yeah
that blues suite
yeah
that peaceful dance
inside a raging tornado
we call
love

Saturday, June 6, 2020
5:37am

I WISH I KNEW HOW IT WOULD FEEL TO BE FREE

You, you may say I'm a dreamer
But I'm not the only one
–JOHN LENNON, "Imagine"

"I always used to tell myself that I was never the type to be a dreamer. I'm the type to be realistic."
–CARDI B

DREAM #1

I went through, in the year 2018, a series of nonstop and overwhelming spiritual and emotional crises that I shall never forget for the rest of my days on this earth. I hate to sound overly dramatic but, yo, ish was mad real, and mad crazy, and made me question why—at times—I was even still alive. Yes, I once again battled the life-long sickness of depression. Yes, it felt like my soul was constantly being punched and bruised by none other than a brass-knuckled Satan. So, when I say "spiritual," I mean to say that my soul was tormented, put on blast, and it felt like I had been dropped off in hell, the hell that those Black holy roller churches my mother and Aunt Cathy and Cousin Anthony and I attended way back, where they preached and sung about hell endlessly, loudly, uncomfortably—where, if you lived a life of sin, of evil, of no-goodness, then you were doomed to be there in that fiery pit, forever and ever, no escaping this whatsoever. Matter of fact, as I struggled to get through 2018, I had many conversations with God... my ancestors... the universe... any and all, asking what I could have possibly done to fall so hard... so fast... so painfully. That is why I will always remember 2018 as absolutely one of the most terrible and most humbling years of my entire life. I should have known it was going to be highly problematic—difficult, frustrating, maddening, harsh—when my wife Jinah and I made the fateful decision to honeymoon on the island of St. Thomas in the U.S. Virgin Islands in late December of 2017, through early January of 2018. Do not get me wrong, the U.S. Virgin Islands, a so-called American "territory," is a place I've always wanted to visit, was spectacularly beautiful; and the place where we stayed offered majestic views of water, land, sky, what truly felt like paradise... or heaven. But only three months prior to that, Hurricane Maria had destroyed, with an unrelenting fury, huge parts of St. Thomas.

We heard stories of whole families sucked by the hurricane from their houses, their bodies ricocheting to-and-fro in the mighty storm. There were the fallen trees, the cars flipped over or flattened, the broken or missing traffic lights, the birds and dogs and cats and other local animals who moved or flew tentatively, for fear of another powerful storm invading their lives anew. There were the apartments and resorts, like the one at which we stayed, that felt like abandoned ghost towns —hardly anyone there—minimal staff milling about, just re-opened, the one economy that supports this and other island nations: tourism, a faint memory of what it had been. There were the mosquitos, lots and lots of mosquitos, who bit and tore into the flesh of my wife and me with no remorse, in the daytime, especially at night, leaving large bumpy gashes on our legs, on our arms, across our bodies, markings that would stay with us for months to come, as a symbol of how badly affected the ecosystem was. And there was that one church that stood, proudly, solemnly, in its refusal to go down with the hurricane, except for the fact that its entire face had been blown off, and it appeared, atop a hill, like a lonely reminder of what must have been a mighty congregation with a mighty preacher—person and a mighty choir, together, swaying with their sweat—soaked souls and their sweat—soaked bibles, praying to God, to Jesus, the way those churches did that I grew up in; anything, yes Lawd, to save us, to save our souls, from the hell that lurks within, the hell that lurks without, except God, nor Jesus, had an answer for a hurricane that stripped that church of its face and made the entire island feel like a death march, or a muted tropical cemetery–

But, we made the best of the trip, that honeymoon, and found ourselves back at the airport, maybe two weeks later, told we could not leave because the flights were backed up, messed up, and our only option would be to fly a six-seater to Puerto Rico, spend a night on that equally hurricane-distressed island, then finally make our way home to New York City. Jinah did not want to do it, was already uncomfortable with flying, and the very thought of being on the smallest plane of her life, with just one pilot, worried her. I was fine with it, had been flying for years, and saw the six-seater as one more great adventure. My wife agreed only because I said we would be good and because we both needed to get home to New York for work and other obligations. But virtually from the moment we were up in the air, she began breathing with great difficulty, anxiety besieging her small frame. I did my best to comfort her, holding her tightly, but by the time we landed Jinah had passed out completely, her eyes rolling in her head, and we had to get a wheelchair, smelling salts, and a medical team to assist her at San Juan Puerto Rico Airport. I was the one scared now, scared that my very new bride might die right there in front of me, and that it was my fault for encouraging her to board that plane. We wheeled Jinah into the airport, through a back entrance not meant for passengers, gave her sip after sip of water, and slowly, very slowly, she came back to consciousness. Relieved and traumatized, I promised Jinah that I would never again ask her to fly on a plane that small.

Out on the sun-kissed streets of Puerto Rico, it was exactly as it was in the U.S. Virgin Islands. And like the Virgin Islands the people of Puerto Rico made a way out of no way. On the one hand Jinah and I felt bad just for visiting these places during these very difficult times. But, on the other, we were glad to be giving both places our money, because we knew that every dime of tourism could help in some way... especially the small businesses we made a point to frequent on both island nations. I had been to Puerto Rico a few times before, but it was Jinah's first visit. We made it a point to walk as much as possible during the one day we spent in Puerto Rico. Made me think of my hometown of Jersey City, and the many Puerto Ricans I loved and admired when I was growing up, the music of salsa, the cultural dish of arroz con pollo, the blending of Spanish with English, the bright and beautiful colors of a proud and beautiful people, the unique offering of what New York-born Puerto Rican poet Tony Medina called "the first truly multicultural people" in the way Puerto Ricans mixed and matched the cultures and histories of Africans,

Europeans, and Indigenous People, to be this rainbow landmass of light skin and dark skin, straight hair and afro-ed hair, thick lips and thick hips and small noses and skinny legs. People like the taxi-driving mother who did not speak English and whose twenty-year-old daughter, fluent in Spanish and English, rode shotgun with mom as my wife and I sat in the backseat. Mother helping daughter pay for college and daughter helping mother with the skills she acquires from that college education. They are Puerto Ricans, yes, but they are also American citizens, just like the people of the U.S. Virgin Islands. And while both people were appreciative of the donations and help and kind words and sorrow songs, underneath, one could feel, was the same frustration many of us feel in Black America: citizens, but not quite citizens, free but not quite free, native people who often feel like we are singing songs in a strange land, in a land that does not really value us as whole human beings.

Yes, I felt like I was home for that one day in P.R., but I also felt something very off in my spirit, in my heart, about the entire experience in both Puerto Rico and the U.S. Virgin Islands, like we probably should not have traveled to either area, except to do relief work. I felt unsettled, honestly, and when we finally got back home to Brooklyn, New York, and got back into the rhythm of our lives, I was reminded why something did not feel right: there was an email lingering, about a lawsuit from a woman in Minnesota named April

Sellers. Back in late October of 2017, during a weekend that my wife and her company were staging her creation, *SHE, a Choreoplay*, for two special performances in New York City, Jinah received a vile, ugly, and hate-filled email from a woman named April Sellers. Mind you, *SHE* speaks to ending violence against women and girls, and to healing and empowerment. But in that email, which was also posted to Jinah's *SHE* Facebook page, Ms. Sellers scolded my wife for being a hypocrite, told her to leave me, a quote unquote wife-beater (I am not, not even close), to cease doing *SHE* as long as she was married to me. Jinah looked at this email while we were in bed on a Saturday morning, the day after the first performance the night before. I noticed that Jinah was trembling, hugely upset. She asked me to read the email. The audacity of it floored me, the hatred spilling, like for real, from the email right into Jinah, and now me. But because I had been in the public eye far longer than my wife, going back to my days on MTV's *The Real World*, and then my work as a writer with Quincy Jones' *Vibe* magazine during that time period, all the way through my two campaigns for Congress in Brooklyn, and so much more, I came to expect perfect strangers to attack me like it was no big deal. They condemned me before emails and social media became the thing. They continue to do so in the age of social media. I deal with death threats, physical stalking, verbal and emotional harassment, and obsessive trolling every single time I appear on a national TV or radio station, particularly from White right-wingers in America. I receive all manner of hate email, hate social media posts, been called a "n****r," a "coon," a "spade," a "jungle bunny," told to "go back to Africa," told to kill myself, you name it. Does not make it any better what my wife received, but my gut reaction was to tell her to ignore it. But I could not ignore it because I saw how much that email affected her. She was deeply distressed by it, and fearful that someone was trying to hurt her, and all her work around *SHE*.

At that moment, I decided to investigate the person named April Sellers. Several Google searches led me to a White sister in Minneapolis, Minnesota, with that name—a dancer and choreographer just like my wife. Could this be her? I wondered, who would send such a hateful, racist, sexist, mean-spirited email? It seemed logical given that she did what my wife did, the same art, the same kind of work around women and gender and dance. And given how insanely racist America has been and had gotten in the era of Donald Trump, liberal or conservative White person, it did not matter. Racism is racism. And Black folks have been conditioned, these past few years to everything from police murders on video, to White people, liberal, conservative, moderate, it does not matter, calling the police on us, for playing basketball too hard with them, for having cook-outs in public spaces, for meeting peacefully at a Starbucks, for taking a nap in the graduate dorm of an Ivy League school at which we were a student. The list is endless, so to my wife and me, it seemed feasible that the April Sellers who sent the hate-filled email to Jinah was the same April Sellers who was a dancer and choreographer in Minnesota.

But it was not something that was front and center in our minds. What was front and center in our minds was *SHE, a Choreoplay*, and that fall of 2017 the explosion of the #MeToo movement, something we could not have predicted when Jinah first conceived of *SHE* in April of 2016. My dear friend and fellow activist Tarana Burke, a Black woman, coined the term "me too" in the mid-2000s as she worked with Black and Latinx young girls in our communities around self-esteem and self-empowerment, and noted that the vast majority were survivors of rape and other acts of sexual violence, usually at the hands of men or boys. Tarana did this work for years quietly, in relative obscurity, until major Hollywood stars began to come forward and assert "me too" in the wake of multiple allegations against famous men like movie mogul Harvey Weinstein. But long before this explosion into the American consciousness, countless women and girls suffered silently, most of their stories never heard. That is why Jinah decided to create *SHE*. My wife thought of *SHE* as strictly a dance piece in 2016, but in doing interviews with various female survivors Jinah decided to ask four of them to be in the very first production of *SHE*, at New York Live Arts, in April of 2016. I agreed to produce *SHE* and helped to promote it.

Little did Jinah and I know that that very first show would turn into a full-fledged play, or what Jinah came to call a choreoplay, and that my wife would wind up staging *SHE* in some form, over the course of two years, at colleges and universities, in various community spaces, and a highly successful Off-Off-Broadway run in the spring of 2017 at HERE Arts Center in Manhattan. Indeed, *SHE* grew so big and so fast, too, thanks to social media, word of mouth, write-ups in places like *The Village Voice* and *The New York Times*, and the very public support of influential women and women's groups like Eve Ensler, Gabrielle Union, Regina King, *Elle* magazine, the National Organization of Women, and the United Nations Women. SHE started with a $5,000 budget at New York Live Arts, and by the time we got to HERE Arts Center it had grown to nearly $100,000. We made the transition from no director to a director, from real women sharing their stories to trained actresses in the roles Jinah conceived, including one character based on Jinah's late grandmother, herself a survivor of childhood sexual abuse. Jinah saw an idea transform into a 21st century version of Eve Ensler's *The Vagina Monologues* remixed with Ntozake Shange's *For Colored Girls Who Have Considered Suicide/ When the Rainbow Is Enuf*. Jinah had conceived something that was her vision, her merging of dance, her craft since she was four years old, with theater and music and film. We worked hard, we worked relentlessly, building *SHE*, building its brand. It was especially powerful to have the talkbacks after each of the fifteen performances at HERE, where we had audiences of every skin color and gender identity, every class and cultural and age background: where a high school boy stood up and said he had never thought about how he treated girls, but now he would; where a woman from California stood up and said she had been carrying around the trauma of her abuser for nearly a decade, and just wanted to release it by screaming, and so Jinah encouraged her to do so, right then and there, and asked the audience to join this woman in screaming, and we did; and there was the last day of the HERE run, a Sunday afternoon, where it was so packed that the extra seats and people standing nearly spilled out of the door—a clear fire hazard. And during that last day, a Black woman raised her hand to speak, and said she was one of the accusers of Bill Cosby, that she did not want to come, but that a friend encouraged her to do so, and she was glad that she did. You could not hear a sound as this woman spoke. She revealed the shame she had carried around for years, of the price she had paid with her life, her career as an actress, because of the towering iconic figure Cosby had been. As she spoke, I thought, as I did at every single performance of *SHE*, of how I had come to this work myself, long before I had met Jinah, in the early 1990s. It was on the heels of my pushing a girlfriend into a bathroom door, during an argument, in July of 1991. I was in my twenties then, a young and confused man-child not sure what to do with the anger, the rage, I seemed to have had been born with, nor the confusion I had about what it was to be a man. I simply knew, in that instance, that I felt powerless as my then-girlfriend challenged me, so I pushed her into that bathroom door, and watched her run, barefoot, out of the apartment, into the Brooklyn streets. I would never again put my hands on a woman in all those years later because women—and men—challenged me in ways that I had never been challenged before, about what I came to call "the incident." About my mistake. To get help immediately, which meant going back to therapy. To get to the root causes of my anger, my rage. To really begin to re-think and re-define manhood. I became aware that I had no real definition of manhood in the first place, that it was merely about power and privilege and all I had been taught, in school, on television, in the movies, in my various religious experiences in college, by other males, here there everywhere. I needed to strip all of that away... a shocking proposition. I had to become, as the Christians say, born again, and I had to begin to walk a different kind of walk. It meant, over time, that I had to write and speak about it, which I did, openly, honestly. It meant that I had to become, over time, an ally to women and girls; and it meant I had to struggle to find a new path, even as I made other "man" mistakes after that incident, although nothing like that previous incident with a woman ever again, as I said.

And I certainly shared all of this from the moment when I met Jinah in June of 2015, who I was, where I had come from, because I have always been honest–brutally honest–about my entire life. Considering this, I felt compelled, too, to find out who April Sellers was who had sent this terrible letter to my wife, hurting Jinah, calling Jinah a "hypocrite," and calling me a "wife-beater." Again, I did several Google searches for April Sellers, and every single one led to April Sellers, dancer and choreographer, in Minnesota. As a result, I texted, called, emailed, and messaged some folks I knew in the Minneapolis-St. Paul area asking if they knew her. People either said they did not, or just never responded. But when one Minnesota-based person, an old writer friend I knew from New York by the name of Rohan Preston said he did know April Sellers personally, in October 2017, I leaped at the opportunity to ask him some questions. My wife and I were in an Uber coming from brunch in Brooklyn when Rohan returned my call. Because I have known him for about 25 years, because folks of my generation like him have literally grown up together since we were young poets, young journalists, and because I knew Rohan's fine work as a cultural critic with the area's daily newspaper, the *Star Tribune*–indeed as one of the leading writers there–I trusted him. I assumed that he, colleague-to-colleague, writer-to-writer, man-to-man, and, honestly, Black person-to-Black person, would tell me the truth. I shared the hateful email with him and told him that

"April Sellers" also posted the note to my wife on Facebook, thereby making it public. Given all we had done around *SHE*, we feared that this person wanted to sabotage and destroy the work by attacking my wife, her integrity, me, my integrity, and our marriage—especially given that we had just gotten married months before, on Saturday, June 10, 2017. As I would later describe in my deposition Rohan said he understood, and as I talked with him in that Uber, he volunteered, privately, that sending the deeply offensive email sounded like something the April Sellers he knew would do, that she had a history of just "going off on people," and that she also had a history of trafficking in the culture of Black people, of other people of color. I trusted Rohan Preston, took his word, implicitly, and because my wife and I endured some unsettling experiences around the *SHE* production—with folks inside and outside the production—I suggested to Jinah that we, two weeks after she had gotten that original email, that we respond with an open letter to April Sellers of Minnesota. And to do so especially since this same Minnesota writer friend had promised me that he would talk with this April Sellers in Minnesota, which I had asked him to do. At that point we felt we had no other choice but to respond with an open letter.

So, we did. We were hurt, we were upset, we were angry. We told Ms. Sellers that we felt her email and Facebook post to Jinah were racist, sexist, and the sign of someone who was very clearly emotionally wounded in some way. We told Ms. Sellers who we really were—our backgrounds, our life work, with links. We told Ms. Sellers we were going to tell a bunch of folks in Minnesota and around the country about her email. But we never did. I never did. I was the writer of the email, Jinah approved of it. We sent it to the email address the original email came from, and we also found an email tied to the April Sellers Dance Collective in Minnesota, and sent it there, too. And in our minds, that was our reply to her email, and it was over. Shortly thereafter, Jinah and I received an email from April Sellers in Minnesota saying we had the wrong person, that she did not know who we were, and asking us to call her. Jinah and I were scared, very scared, to be honest. Based on the original email and Facebook post of that hateful message, we did not know if the author of the email was mentally stable, dangerous, a stalker. Jinah and I agreed it was best not to respond. We did not. We hoped that the matter was closed. This was not the first time that I responded like this to such a message. One of my mentors and sheroes, the legendary feminist scholar Dr. bell hooks, told me years back that sometimes we must respond to craziness, to drama, then let it go. This was how I saw the situation. I will add that not only did we send the open letter to two April Sellers email addresses, but I also pulled up about 35 or so Minneapolis-area email addresses and sent it to those as well, individuals, local media, local arts organizations, local foundations. Some folks I knew, some I did not. Not a single person ever responded, and to this day I do not know if any of them ever even read the open letter. We never—not once—posted the open letter on social media nor did the open letter ever go beyond Minnesota. The April Sellers who responded to us also actually posted what was happening on Facebook, which further deepened our fear of her, our suspicions of her. That same April Sellers sent a second email maybe a week or two later, and we again decided not to respond, hoping that the whole matter would disappear. This time she demanded to know to whom we had sent the open letter. Then a month went by, and we considered the matter over—

But just before Jinah and I were about to leave for our honeymoon in the U.S. Virgin Islands, we both received an email from a lawyer named Aaron Scott with the Minnesota office of a firm called Fox Rothschild saying that we were being sued for $500,000, the complaint referred to me as a "celebrity author," mentioned that I had been a cast member on the first season of MTV's *The Real World* (I mean, that was all the way back in 1992....), talked about how we had damaged April Sellers' reputation, referenced conversations I had had with Minnesota associates, and especially attacked my character, essentially calling me violent, abusive, and more. It was so outlandish that we thought the entire thing was a joke. I could not believe that a serious and professional lawyer would send something like that. We ignored it and went on our honeymoon.

But when we returned from the great adventure that was the U.S. Virgin Islands and Puerto Rico, two harsh realities greeted us: first, that we only had three months to the April 2018 Off-Broadway debut of SHE, and there was suddenly an urgency to get everything set up and going. As I said before, SHE had grown so fast and so big that we now had a production team that totaled at least a dozen people. Add in the six dancers and the cast of four actresses we were set to bring on board, and the team now stretched to nearly 25 people. In hindsight, we were not prepared for this huge a leap in such a short period of time, nor were we ready to take show Off-Broadway in just three months. But as lead producer I thought we could pull it off because we had staged, SHE for two years, we paid every single bill, and every staging ended with more and more people asking to see the production. We felt a great sense of obligation to keep going. Meanwhile, once back home in New York, we got another email from Minnesota attorney Aaron Scott saying we were being sued. This time I decided to get a lawyer in Minneapolis to respond but realized that I did not know any attorneys in that state. I reached out to a few of my associates there to find out about Minnesota lawyers. A few suggestions came back my way. I made the grave mistake of taking the advice of a local Alpha Phi Alpha fraternity brother of mine and going with a Black woman lawyer in the Twin Cities named Karlowba Powell. She sounded qualified enough via telephone, talked much about community, about racism, knew who I was, my name, my work —or at least claimed she did—and pledged to take on the case, for not a lot of money, because she insisted it was a frivolous lawsuit, and would be easily dismissed. My wife and I paid her a retainer, and we went about the business of mounting the Off-Broadway production of *SHE*—

That effort quickly turned into a nightmare. There was fatigue from potential investors given how much they had supported us the past two years to get *SHE* this far, and fatigue from the small-donor community because we had constantly asked for support, and for the first time we got responses like "I've donated already," repeatedly. I confronted the stubborn reality that I alone as the producer was responsible for paying the salaries of these nearly 25 people, and not all the money we needed—a whopping $500,000 budget—had been raised as yet, because I had run into the holiday season in late 2017 first, then my need to be on the road in January 2018 doing more Dr. King holiday speeches than I had anticipated. And, truthfully, I was overwhelmed and intimidated by the sheer enormity of *SHE, a Choreoplay*, at this point. I was still a new theater producer, still learning the ropes on the fly, and simply had been using whatever skill sets I had to produce, non-traditionally, this very non-traditional theater piece. But I could no longer rely on that. I had to raise all the money... and quickly. The cracks began to show when we had to borrow $30,000 from my wife's grandmother just to get the show bonded as an Off-Broadway production. Doubly so when I bounced a few of the first checks to the dancers and actresses after starting rehearsals. And I began to stall the rest of the team regarding payments, because the fundraising was not going as quickly as I would have liked. I carried all of this on my shoulders. Meanwhile, our Minnesota lawyer continually said, in January, in February, in March, and in April, that "this frivolous lawsuit will get dismissed," but she also kept asking for more money—money that we did not have. But we scraped together coins and paid our Minnesota lawyer whatever we could, and told her, Karlowba Powell, to please handle the lawsuit, as we were dealing with the monumental task of keeping *SHE, a Choreoplay* alive for its Off-Broadway debut. One day in March I was assured by a major Hollywood figure of support, for at least half of the budget. That was the blessing we needed. But then this individual stalled, disappeared, re-appeared, disappeared again, and finally asked, between production meetings for one of their television projects, if I could send them our banking information for a wire. I was thrilled... overjoyed. And then they asked for it a second time, and I got nervous, but I sent it yet again. Then I waited. And I waited. And I waited. And when the money finally came it was only for a couple of thousand dollars. I was devastated... utterly defeated. I do not know if I cried or not in that very moment, but I do know I was terrified... terrified of having to tell my wife what happened... terrified of having to tell everyone that the production was indeed in trouble, big trouble. In desperation, I reached out to people in panic, which turned off some previous large donors, because no one wants to support anything that appears to be crumbling. Every single emotional issue I have ever suffered re-surfaced because of this crisis around *SHE*. I became distant from the entire production team, and my wife, and the cast, and began to isolate myself. I cursed myself loudly and often for miscalculating the enormity of the problem with the financing. My self-esteem reverted to where it has been for much of my life—a tragic conflict between confidence and a most cruel brand of self-sabotage and self-pity. I began to lose sleep, night upon night of sleep, I felt the stress growing inside of me like the blood-stripping horror from some movie thriller. My demons—every single one of them—shadow-boxed with me, with Jesus, with God, with Satan, with anyone who dared to come into my space to offer a solution. I found myself shamelessly begging people for help, including those who did not truly believe in me, in my wife, in the vision of *SHE*. I listened to these people, as I was begging, interrupt me, to tell me what we should be doing with *SHE*, how badly we had screwed up, without ever offering any sincere help whatsoever. One historic African American theater company went so far as to tell us they were going to work with us, then backed out, and scolded us as they abandoned us. Slowly, one by one, members of the production team began to do work stoppages, in March of 2018, the set designer and others, until they were paid, and regardless of our history of paying everyone. Things fell apart daily, and it finally hit the fan when a production team member, who had been with us since the very first show, disrupted the entire production by openly questioning what was happening. Jinah and I were floored, because they knew our hearts, knew our souls, knew that for two years we had paid everyone on the team, while never taking a single dime in payment for ourselves. We were distraught because they had told us how much *SHE* had affected them... how much they believed in it, but now it seemed the only thing that mattered was the money... not the mission. They quit one by one, the set designer and a production team member, with others threatening to quit every day. I tried one last Hail Mary to save the show, talking with a production consultant to come aboard, to see what she thought could get us to opening night. But on a Sunday morning she called me and said after reviewing everything, like everything, that our wisest decision was to shut the production down completely. It felt like something crawled inside my body and set my soul afire. But she was right. And later that afternoon I faced the onerous task of informing the director, my wife Jinah, and the entire cast of *SHE* that the show would not go on. I felt like a complete and utter failure, that I had let them all down, like I had let down all the people who had already purchased tickets and who were going to purchase tickets. They cried, I cried, we all cried, on that Sunday afternoon in the rehearsal space. I experienced failure previously, lost large amounts of money, and lived with little or no money. But because *SHE* is about ending violence against women and girls, about healing and empowerment, I, as a man, as a male ally, felt an incredible amount of shame and guilt, as if I had shirked my responsibility to make this production happen. And I felt, whether it was true or not, that many on the team were eyeballing me, were questioning me, were looking at me as a liar, as a loser, as someone not to be trusted ever again. Whether true or not this is what I felt, and for the next two months or so after that fateful Sunday in April of 2018, I could hardly get out of bed, to function in any meaningful way. Yes, I sank into a deep depression, my wife Jinah did, too, and we were miserable, together, and toward each other. It felt as though *SHE* was over forever, and we both, somewhere in our now ultra-paranoid minds, believed that. We owed a debt of $200,000 because of the postponement, with no idea how we were going to pay off those production costs. Delaying the Off-Broadway debut neither stopped nor erased that bleeding, or the pain of it all.

DREAM # 2

The summer of 2018 was pure hell. My wife and I had no money and the *SHE* $200,000 debt hovered over us. Plus, as we were dealing with the *SHE* implosion and the Minnesota lawsuit I did not hear my accountant telling me that I needed to respond to the IRS quickly. If I did not, the agency would place a levy on my bank account, my sources of income, everything. I did not, so the IRS did, and my wife and I were shell-shocked because not only did we have the *SHE* debt and the Minnesota lawsuit, but now my sources of income had been methodically shut down by the IRS. Thus, it felt like we did absolutely nothing in New York City that summer of 2018 except mope around. I wondered, often, through that sadness, about the theater industry in New York, the theater industry in general, why it was so hard for folks to produce theater, why there were so few theater producers of color, Black, any people not White. For sure, of the forty or so Broadway theater producers, there was only one Black team, a woman and a man. We had gotten *SHE* this far because of small donors, because of a few large donors and by being creative financially with what we had, never relying on the system in place, or even the foundation world for help. It was during these dark times, that depression hounded me everywhere in our tiny Brooklyn Heights apartment, grabbed me about the neck and held me in a chokehold, and made me feel as worthless as I had ever felt in my life. During this period, I contemplated, yes, loudly in my bed, suicide, ending my life, and posted cryptic messages on social media. People who expected to see positive words from me for many years found themselves stunned. Some did not know what to say and said nothing. Others tried to send me loving, affirming thoughts, but these words meant nothing to me. I simply struggled to find the will to live, to be, for myself, for my wife, for my ailing mother, for anyone who valued me more than I valued myself in that moment. But as I sat in our apartment or walked the streets of Brooklyn Heights where we lived at the time, I pondered what might be different had I been more effective in engaging large investors and donors... had we paused long enough to apply for a few grants... had we rubbed elbows more with the theater-producing community. Those doubts did not help us in the short term, but they rang through my brain like a massive bell, and I found myself hypersensitive to everything. Those insults coupled with viral videos of indignity after indignity visited upon Black folks just because they were Black, videos of Black men, Black women, Black children being harassed, beaten up, shot, murdered by police seemingly everywhere. The daily barrage of Donald Trump, his red-meat viciousness to all people, but especially to people of color. His nonstop disses of Barack Obama, his predecessor. The license Trump's very presence in the White House seems to give certain segments of White America, consciously, subconsciously, liberal, conservative, moderate, that they can say and do anything to Black people, to people of color, at any time and in any place, without fear of consequences. Like the way some White people in Brooklyn Heights would try to walk through my wife and me on the street as if we were not there on the sidewalk with them. Like the way some White people in Brooklyn Heights would assume, because my wife was walking our two dogs, that she must be a dogwalker, or a housekeeper or nanny, not a resident in that 'hood. Like the way some White people in our Brooklyn Heights high-rise building would never speak to us, the lone all-Black couple in the 30-plus floors of that apartment house, because they had been conditioned to view Black people as security... maintenance... the help...

And like the way my wife and I felt, in June of 2018, when that White male lawyer from Minnesota, Aaron Scott, aggressively questioned us, at our deposition in New York City, about our incomes, about what insurance we might have for *SHE*, our theater production, when there was none; and like the way Aaron Scott got the Minnesota judge overseeing the lawsuit, Karen Janisch, to sanction us monetarily—time and again—for things that we did not understand, or were explained to us incompletely by Karlowba Powell, our first Minnesota attorney. She raised serious doubts about the case, which gave us comfort the case would be dismissed, yet it continued and cost us more and more money, and we didn't understand why it kept going. So even when my wife and I did manage to earn a few dollars that summer, it either went to sanctions or to that first Minnesota attorney while we struggled to eat day to day, to cover basic bills, and to pay our rent on time. In the midst of the depression, debt, drought, and disorder, I began feeling a wicked sensation that something bad was going to happen. It was similar to how I felt when I first agreed to move to Brooklyn Heights the previous summer: thinking that I might get arrested or killed because I am a Black man in an area with only a handful of Black people—especially after business hours, especially at night. I experienced paranoia, self-doubt, trepidation, and, yes, fear, culminating in late August of 2018, with a rapid and impatient knock on our door. My wife was not home, just me. I found myself hesitant to answer the door at first. It brought back memories of the South Carolina stories I heard of my mother and her three sisters and brother and their father and mother, how when someone would knock on the door, they would get suddenly quiet and still, not sure what threat or danger might be lurking on the other side of that door. When my mother and two of her sisters migrated North, to Jersey City, New Jersey, where I was born and raised, that fear and loathing came with them. And my ma and I would do the exact same thing, be quiet and still. So, I stood there in that Brooklyn Heights apartment for what felt like an eternity debating whether I should utter these three words or not: "Who is it?" Finally, I did—

Turns out it was the Black woman property manager and the Puerto Rican live-in super. The property manager was nervous, and I wondered why she was there, and with the super, too. She asked me if I or anyone in my family were military veterans. I was confused. Military veterans? She asked again if I or anyone in my family were military veterans. Was this a trick question, and better yet, why were the two of them at our door asking that question, of all questions? Then it got weirder. The property manager and the super abruptly left when I finally blurted out "No...." I could hear them taking the stairs instead of the elevator down several flights.

Perplexed, I put on my sneakers and took the elevator to the floor where the property-management office was. There they were, the property manager and the super, looking very uncomfortable when I walked in. I asked what was going on... why had they come to my apartment. The property manager finally said it was because our rent was late. Well, our rent was late all summer because we had no money because of the *SHE* debt, the Minnesota lawsuit, the IRS levy, the lack of work for me as a speaker with colleges gone for the summer and bills just piling up. I still was not clear why they came to the door with that question, when the property manager called or emailed us, mostly email, previously. She muttered something about management policy. I did not believe this.

This sat with me for about a week, into early September. It truly bothered me. Did they do this to the White tenants in the building when their rent was late? Did the White tenants always receive threatening legal notices and eviction notices, as we seemed to get every month? Did the White tenants have to pay a couple of extra hundred dollars whenever their rent was late like ours? Did they ever go knock on the doors of the White tenants to ask them questions about military service, to inquire about the rent? I decided to call the law firm that represented the building, and sure enough a paralegal there, a young White woman whose name I looked up, told me that knocking on folks' doors should always be the last resort, that they should have just sent an email. My wife and I were mystified and bothered by this information. On Wednesday, September 5, 2018, around midday, while I worked with the assistant that Jinah and I shared, I went to the property-manager's office to let her know that I had spoken with their law firm. She was hella defensive—short, abrasive, and acted as if I had violated some imaginary rule. Flabbergasted, I went back to the lounge where my assistant and I were working, where I was signing copies of my 13th and newest book, since I was scheduled to do a big public event with White anti-racist activist and scholar Tim Wise the next day, at the New York Society for Ethical Culture on Manhattan's Upper West Side. The super came into the lounge to look at something that needed to be repaired. He and I had always been cool, always friendly, so I tried to have a conversation with him about the apartment visit the week before. Much to my surprise he had a foul attitude and switched the subject to my "running my business" in the lounge, which he called "illegal." Stunned, I wondered what was happening. Our conversation turned heated. An older White woman sitting in the lounge, who previously made it clear that she did not care for me or my assistant, a young Latinx woman, slammed her laptop shut, stood up dramatically, and said, very loudly, "He acts like this is his personal lounge," in my direction. This was the furthest thing from the truth, I tried to reason with the older woman, but she just huffed and puffed her way out of the lounge. I looked at my assistant, she looked at me, both of us stunned. There was one Black male employee in the building, part of the custodial staff, who kept me abreast of what was really going down with that apartment house. We agreed that the Black woman property manager was doing all she could not to be Black, and he said to me, after that lounge encounter with the super, that the super really did not do much work in the building, treated Black and Latinx maintenance staff in a condescending manner, and he too thought he was better than them. I told my assistant that she could leave early, and I found myself in the hallway corridor outside the lounge, near the elevators talking with this maintenance worker. At some point the property manager and super came by again and the super and I exchanged words right by the property manager's office. Panicked, she tried to pull the super into the office then looked me in the eyes and said, "I am going to call the police on you." My spontaneous words back to her: "What an Uncle Tom you are, threatening to call the police on a Black man who has not done anything other than challenge you two for lying about building policy." Her eyes bulged and she slammed and locked the door as if I was some sort of monster they were escaping. The maintenance worker and I and some outside Black male workers, who were there to fix the heating and cooling system, chatted by the elevators about what just went down. We all agreed it was nonsense, blown out of proportion. The super came out of the office, squeezed by us, and we exchanged words again. Still beefing, the two of us walked together through the exit door heading downstairs to the lobby. In that stairwell we shoved each other a bit, but that was it. I immediately regretted even getting involved with him like that. Something told me to tell the security guard on duty in the lobby that I needed to call the police. First, I dialed the security phone, then changed my mind and called 911 on my cellphone. I had seen this play out too many times in my life as a Black male—a Black man or Black boy is immediately accused of being the instigator, the perpetrator, the one who is blamed for whatever goes down. About fifteen minutes later, four police officers showed up. Two were White, one was Black, and one was Asian. By this time the Black woman property manager was downstairs, and she insisted that I had done something to the super in the stairwell. With no cameras at all in the stairwell, there was no proof of anything, simply her version of the story. The officers first talked with me and I gave them my side of the story. They spent what felt like an hour speaking outside with the super. I wondered why it took so long to resolve such a straightforward matter. We had a dispute and it was over. I called the cellphone of the regional manager for the building —a White woman. She immediately acted as the judge and jury, furious that I had the nerve to call her, when what I was trying to do was resolve the situation. She told me that I should never call her again and hung up the phone. So, I sat and waited. When the officers finally came in, they said the super was pushing hard to have me arrested, which left me aghast. According to the officer, he made all kinds of accusations. That I attacked him. That I reached into the equipment belt around his waist, took his hammer out, and struck him on the head with it. The officers told me what they told him: if we arrest one of you, then we will have to arrest the other one. The matter was over, the officers told us to keep our distance from each other, and they left.

The next day, Thursday, September 6th, I woke up with that wicked sense of impending doom pulsating in my bones. As I said, I had the big event with Tim Wise that night to promote my new essay collection, but that morning I had to go to Manhattan to be on the Sirius XM Satellite show of Sway, the legendary TV and radio personality. One of his co-hosts is Heather B, my castmate from our original season of MTV's *The Real World*. It was like a family reunion up in that piece, and it felt good with us vibing, me, Sway, and Heather, about our collective MTV days (Sway came to prominence there with many great interviews, including one with President Obama); and it was especially mad cool to field calls from listeners, including ones where folks were complaining about the mostly Black professional football players and their protests. I still had the nagging feeling when I left the studio and hopped the subway train back to Brooklyn. Something told me to go to the 84th Precinct in the Fort Greene section of Brooklyn—right around the corner from where I lived before the move to Brooklyn Heights—to file a complaint against the super in my building. Why? Because I have had enough experiences as a Black man to understand our vulnerability in this country where we can be stopped, pulled over, beaten up, assaulted, brutalized, arrested, locked up, killed at any time and any place. I needed to put my story on the record. Something told me to do this, so I did.

Then I made the slow walk from Fort Greene back to our Brooklyn Heights residence. I tried to rid my mind of anything but the event that night with Tim Wise. When I arrived at the building the energy got even stranger as I walked through the lobby, to the elevator, got on, and headed to our apartment. My wife had stepped out, so I was home alone with our two dogs. Jinah had left the television on for the pets, as she always does, and I vaguely heard some things about Donald Trump, but mostly blocked it and him from my mind. I was hungry and not quite sure what I was going to do for lunch. I was in the bedroom milling about when, about fifteen minutes later, I heard a heavy thump on the door. Again, I froze, wondering who that could be in the middle of the day. Once more I was not sure if I should even answer the door, and it felt like my feet were stuck in quicksand. Somehow, I got my feet to move and I walked slowly to the door and asked, "Who is it?" From the other side of the door a woman's voice said, "It's the police, please open the door." I felt my heart plunge down south into my knees. Once more I was frozen. Then, again: "It's the police, please open the door." I did not know what to do, did not want to open the door, but what choice did I have, really? I opened it halfway, and the police officers, a Black woman followed by a Black man, pushed their way into the apartment. The woman officer, for whatever reason, was exceptionally antagonistic. I tried to talk with her and all she kept saying was "You are under arrest." And she told me the building's super, property manager, and regional property manager had called the police, demanding my arrest. I stammered, first, that the police had just been to the building last night, and left, telling us to stay away from each other. And, second, that I had just come from the precinct at which the officers were based, the 84th, and had filed a report. The woman officer said it did not matter, they had no record of that, that I needed to put my shoes on and be prepared to get handcuffed and escorted downstairs. As I stood there feeling totally demoralized, my wife arrived, the dogs barked wildly, and, out in the hallway, in a white dress shirt and blue jeans, my hands were put behind my back and my wife was told I was being taken in for "assault." In that moment, as the two officers put me on the elevator, I wished that I had a hoodie on my head to conceal my identity. When we got to the lobby, I observed the Black woman property manager and the Latinx super standing with smirks on their faces as the two officers led me from the building. I wanted to give them the middle finger but that was not happening with handcuffs. For a brief moment, I was terrified to step through the doors of the building into the daylight heart of Brooklyn Heights for fear that someone would recognize me, take a picture or video, post to social media that I, Kevin Powell, was being walked from a building, across the street, for what felt like an hour, to a police squad car, in handcuffs. The officers told me to duck down, just like in the news clips, just like in the movies or TV shows, and to push my way into the back seat, with my hands behind my back. One officer drove while the other sat in the back with me as we made our way to the 84th Precinct for my booking. A Brooklynite for over half my life, I never felt my home borough move as slowly as it did in the back of that patrol car. When we finally arrived at the station, the officers pulled me out of the car and marched me through the back entrance of the precinct house. Various cops of different backgrounds glanced at me matter-of-factly, the routine of seeing prisoners brought in as commonplace as swigging on a Coke or taking a drag on a cigarette. When we got to the desk, I saw one of the police officers from the night before who had told the super and me to keep our distance, a young Chinese American man. Clearly a rookie he appeared genuinely surprised to see me there in handcuffs. He asked me what happened, and I told him they called the cops again, for no reason. The officer was so green that he was speechless, and his heart popped through his eyes, his sorrow for me mad real.

The two cops who arrested me said some words to an older White cop behind the big counter, then brought me into a back room where they fingerprinted me, took my mug shot, and put me in a holding cell. My wife showed up to the precinct to try to get me out, to help me, to do whatever she could do. At that moment, the Black female officer softened, recognized me, and said that she remembered attending some of the community events that I produced in New York City. She looked sincerely embarrassed and guilty for arresting me so summarily. She took my cellphone to my wife and gave Jinah the message to call a lawyer I knew. When she returned the officer apologized for incarcerating me but said there was nothing she could do now that I was booked into the system. I asked her if I might be able to get released shortly so that I could make my big book launch event with Tim Wise that night in Manhattan. She said that would not be happening. My heart sank. I asked if I could make my one phone call to my wife. The officer said that I could. I told Jinah what to tell my book publicist and Tim Wise: that I had a very serious emergency, something beyond my control, and that I apologized from the bottom of my heart. And to tell the same to the Barnes & Noble folks, and to the people at The New York Society for Ethical Culture, who booked its space to us. I was devastated. I had never spent a night in jail in my life, and now here I was. I was put back in the holding cell, and I suddenly found myself curiously and instantly hungry and thirsty, I do not know why. But that is what I felt in that precinct jail.

In the other holding cell was a young Black man who was only about 21 years old, young enough to be my son. But he already had a lengthy record of identity theft, due to his poverty and unstable living situation. We sat there for several hours, we talked some, we did not speak at all, essentially left in that back room alone, until nightfall, with one officer or another periodically coming in to say that we would be transported to Central Booking in Downtown Brooklyn over at 120 Schermerhorn "soon." During this long wait, my mind began playing tricks on me. After being falsely accused of assault—a felony charge—would they take me to Rikers Island, the infamous New York prison? What if I received jail time? What if the police officers or the corrections officers attacked me and beat me to a bloody mess? Worse yet, what if they beat me badly, then say I resisted arrest, and I died in their custody? Kevin, how did you wind up here? What if the media finds out, what if they wait for you to be taken from this holding cell to the car outside, to head to jail for the night? What if what if what if—

Finally, about five or six hours after I arrived at the 84th Precinct, the young inmate and I were told to get up, that we were heading out. They placed our hands behind our backs and handcuffed us, then led us through the precinct rear entrance to an awaiting squad car. We both struggled to get ourselves into the cramped back seat, and there was simply no way to sit with your hands cuffed behind you, without being in great discomfort to the point of pain. The siren blared and the lights flashed and again my beloved Brooklyn streets moved like molasses. The two officers riding up front parked the car and took us out. We crossed the street and found ourselves being led down a slope into Central Booking. Once inside, they placed us in a cell with some other men, and locked the thick white door shut, with a thud. I looked around me, at the inmates in this new cell, at those going through the process. The vast majority were Black or Latinx of disparate ages and generations, but all men of color. Like the 84th Precinct holding cell it was damp and freezing at Central Booking. I folded myself in half, standing, sitting down, whatever I could do to gain warmth. None of it worked. Then we were rotated out of that holding cell and lined up against a wall—like cattle, or slaves—each of us handcuffed, some handcuffed together as if they had been captured and arrested together. Again, we were screened, photographed, fingerprinted, and our private parts were checked. Round and round we went, until we got to a point where we were asked, one by one, if we needed to see a doctor. I thought to say yes but was scared that taking me to the hospital would extend my jail stay. I said I was fine. We were led to huge holding cells that could easily accommodate two or three dozen men. These large holding cells reeked of urine and feces with discarded food everywhere, and roaches—lots and lots of them—eagerly nibbling and biting at the discarded food. Clumps of feces floated at the top of the unflushed toilet—open, with no covering. If you had to go you just had to go. I wondered where we were going to sleep, if they would feed us at all, if there would be water, at the least. I asked a few officers if I could have my one phone call. They said where we were now there were no phone calls. We clearly were underground, in a bottomed-out dungeon. There were no clocks, no windows, just us, and the police and the corrections officers. Anything could happen at any time, it felt that volatile, that violent, that dangerous.

We were told to line up, both large holding cells, one-by-one our names were called, and we were led down a corridor with a sharp left turn where there were more cells, smaller, but like five of them, where we were deposited, one-by-one. Five of us sat in my cell and we each held faint hope that our names would be called before the late-night court session was over. I bowed my head, closed my eyes tightly, and prayed to God that I would hear my name. As the clock went past midnight, then one in the morning, I realized that I had no other choice but to do what everyone else did in each of the cells: find a part of a bench or floor on which to sleep.

I did not sleep that night. Inmates babbled loudly. One or more yelled at the correction officers every half hour or so asking for the time, or for a cup for water, or one of the two sandwiches available to us: peanut butter and jelly, or ham and cheese. Being a vegan, I drank water. And I thought of my wife and how terrified she must have been with her husband in jail for no good reason, and how she surely was not sleeping because she knew, as did I, that I could come back to her dead, in a body bag. I shoved that thought from my brain as best I could, engaged in periodic conversations with one cellmate or another, and listened to quite a few, through the wee hours of the morning. They talked about their cases as if they were seasoned attorneys. Some were charged with burglary, others with domestic violence, including one gentleman with a record of battering women in all five of New York City's boroughs, and Westchester County, just north of The Bronx, too. There were petty criminals and jaywalkers. There were those who had failed to pay child support and those caught driving with suspended licenses. Some, like me, came in handcuffs by themselves. Others came in a chain gang of five, six, or more, handcuffed together, jarring my worst memories of this country's treatment of Black and Brown men, of people of color, from slavery forward. The sight of that sickened me to the core. There were men who were clearly college-educated, like me, and others who more than likely never finished high school. There were men in a jail for the first time in their lives, like me. There was the one elder Black man in his 60s who I learned later had suffered a horrendous seizure: wriggling and gagging and drooling on the floor uncontrollably like an untamed bull before we got to these final cells for the night. It took four or five officers to detain him and remove him immediately to the nearest hospital. There were men who faked being ill because they knew the hospital would give them a bed for the night, a meal or two, and they would still be back in time for court. There was the young man I counseled on the spot—a model and actor—in jail because his baby's mother had called the police on him, locking him up a second time because of their tumultuous relationship. There was the one man in my cell who talked with me about his history of unrepentant violence and at that moment it became clear to me that this man did not need jail but a serious mental health intervention, and I hoped he would not attack me while we shared that cell. Luckily, he talked himself into a deep sleep on the cold, dusty floor. There were men who were in jail so frequently that this felt like home, including some who had purposely gotten themselves arrested, because they knew at least inside jail or prison they would have food and shelter on the regular. And there was the one man, put in a cell by himself a bit away from the rest of us, who screamed all night, his cries piercing the stink air of this underground dungeon, and no amount of howling back by his fellow inmates, or the police, or the correction officers, would quiet this man. He was determined to be heard; he was determined to be free in his own way–

Around six in the morning, we were told to get up. I smelled my own body odor born of a day and night in custody, I tasted the nasty flavor of my bad breath, and I felt the thick wrinkles of my white shirt. We were lined up, again. I was so used to being handcuffed at this point that I instinctively put my hands behind my back before I was even asked. And then we were marched to the large holding cells and had to wait there until court opened at 9am. Why did they have us up at 6am if we had to wait three hours in different cells? Nothing was ever really explained to us; we were just told to do this to do that.

My name was not called until about 10am, four hours later. I and other inmates were led upstairs to just outside another holding room where we were lined up again, our handcuffs were removed, and we were instructed to walk in. I was told this was the final cell or room before we would see the judge. In a section of that room, we could talk with legal aid lawyers for our cases on a phone with glass separating inmates and lawyers. A nice young White woman attorney called my name at some point to come and talk with her. I was so desperate to speak with anyone who was not a prisoner or a cop or corrections officer that I speed-talked what happened to me, told her who I was, told her what a great injustice and violation this was, and she was immediately sympathetic. I thanked her profusely for helping me and I asked if I would be getting out. She said that I would be. I sighed a heavy relief. I waited and waited some more, until nearly twelve noon, and I suddenly feared that I would not see the judge before the lunch break or, worse, since it was now a Friday, I would be stuck there over the weekend, until the following Monday. But, finally, my name was called, before lunch, and I and other men were lined up, handcuffed, and walked down the long corridor to what was the courtroom. Until that moment, I had no idea that the court was in the very same building as where we had been imprisoned overnight. Once inside the courtroom I strained my eyes looking for my wife, for the lawyer I asked my wife to call, someone, anyone I knew. No familiar face was there–

Now before the judge my legal aid lawyer spoke on my behalf, and then the Brooklyn District Attorney's Office gave the charge. My physically and emotionally drained body flinched and recoiled at the lies about what allegedly happened, but I said nothing. Then it was over, I was told to stay away from the super, and to be back in court in a few weeks. After a short wait for paperwork, I walked out of the courtroom, nodding my head at men who had been there with me overnight, hoping I would never see any of them ever again in this way. Into the crisp September air of Brooklyn, I made a beeline straight to Perelandra, one of my favorite organic food markets, to get something to eat. I was beyond starving. Just as I was at the counter getting ready to pay, my wife ran into the store in tears and into my arms. It felt like I had not seen her in years. She hugged me tightly, and I her, right in that store, not wanting to let each other go. Jinah said she was not at court because they had given her the runaround about when I would be brought before the judge, and she simply did not know what time to be there, and she was so anxious that she just walked around the area in an inconsolable haze of dread. Beyond elated and relieved to be with my wife again, I just wanted to take a shower to wash away that ugly jail experience, and to go to sleep–

DREAM #3

Somewhere after my arrest in early September of 2018, which I feel was partially brought on by the unbearable stress and toxic energy accumulated from the *SHE* cancellation and its $200,000 debt, the never-ending IRS levy, and the lawsuit in Minnesota, my wife and I finally decided to break from our original attorney, Karlowba Powell, and retained Lee Hutton to represent us there. Things changed for the better immediately. Lee possessed the qualities lacking in our previous counsel's handling of our case: confidence, experience, and knowledge about all kinds of cases... and the ability to explain things simply to my wife and to me. His analysis of the situation shocked us. First, the original lawyer never communicated to my wife or me, not via email, not via telephone call, that a trial date had been set for December 2018. Second, he believed that Attorney Karlowba Powell mishandled the case: it was a frivolous lawsuit that should have and could have been dismissed had she done a better job. Equally upsetting, she never bothered to tell us that she had been temporarily suspended in 2017 because of a prior legal blunder. Finally, it was Lee Hutton who had to inform Jinah and me that we had a September mediation, as we were not told by Attorney Powell neither by email nor telephone of a definite mediation date. My wife and I scrambled to get to Minnesota, to meet Lee for the first time, to sit down with the other side and see if they would accept an apology. I had to borrow money for this trip but was too ashamed to tell anyone what the loans were for. This was Jinah's first time in Minneapolis-St. Paul, and neither one of us was happy about being there under these circumstances. The mediator, an elderly, retired White male judge, admitted that he was a friend of the judge assigned to the case. As he had done at the deposition in New York City in June, the lawyer for April Sellers, Aaron Scott, proceeded to go off on me, my character, like it was no big deal. After all I had been through in 2018, I pulled no punches with Aaron Scott. At the height of my frustration during the mediation I labeled him an opportunist, a money-grabber, and said that I felt this whole thing was racist, the lawsuit and the attacks on me. Rattled, the mediator called for a break in the proceedings. April Sellers, looking mad shook, reacted as if I were some sort of big Black boogey-man, all barely six feet and one hundred sixty pounds of me. She and Aaron Scott were ordered to a separate room for the remainder of the mediation. But no real mediation took place. We tried to reach practical and reasonable solutions, but the other side rejected our offers. Thus, one of the most bizarre chapters of my life was now heading to a December 2018 trial for Jinah and me there in Minnesota. In the intervening months our financial situation worsened... if that were possible. The IRS battled with my accountant and tax attorney over demands for an outrageous monthly payment. I reeled like a punch-drunk aging boxer as the time for the Minnesota trial approached. Shortly before the trip my wife made several visits to the doctor, including one to a hospital. Among other stress-induced ailments, she suffered an outbreak of shingles, which rarely occurs in younger people. I tried to ignore the fact that I barely slept and experienced foul and frightening nightmares. Mysteriously, my bladder became so weak that I went to the bathroom every ten minutes. As the fateful day of the Minnesota trial approached, Jinah and I could not afford our plane tickets, our hotel room for the expected three-day trial, or money for us to eat while there. With our flight scheduled for 7pm that night, I desperately reached out to as many folks as I could and told them I needed to handle a "family emergency" in Minnesota, and that we needed to borrow coins to get there as fast as possible. Via Cash App, Venmo, and PayPal, a few friends from different parts of the country came through for us. Depressed, I feared that we would not be able to get to Minnesota and would lose the case by default. But we made it... barely.

The next morning, we met our attorney Lee Hutton and his law clerk Madelyn Buxton, a wonderfully progressive young White sister, outside the courtroom. We did not know what to expect. From the moment that we retained Lee back in September, he cautioned us that the manner in which the case had been managed meant that we now faced an uphill battle. Attorney Karlowba Powell never even took a deposition from April Sellers, the plaintiff, a standard procedure in such lawsuits. Once inside the courtroom, we met Judge Karen Janisch, a White woman, who had penalized us financially during the summer months, at the prompting of Aaron Scott. A Republican, Ms. Janisch was first a trial attorney then general counsel to Tim Pawlenty, a past Republican governor of Minnesota, who appointed her to the bench. At our table sat Lee, Madelyn (or "Maddy" as we called her), Jinah, and me. Across the aisle from us we saw the two White male attorneys, Aaron Scott and Peter Stiteler, and the White female plaintiff, April Sellers. A third lawyer, a Black woman named Rashanda Bruce, sat behind them. Our side noticed immediately that Ms. Bruce was the one setting everything up, carrying in most of the boxes at the start of each day and out at the end of each day, as if she were not a lawyer at all, but the help—a stunning visual of racism and sexism. It appeared that Aaron Scott was responding to my statement at the September mediation that I felt racist energy from this lawsuit. So, he put a Black woman on the team, albeit one not treated as an equal to the White men. On our side, Lee made sure that Maddy sat right next to him at our table and consulted her on everything. During the trial, we noted that whenever the judge called the lawyers to the chambers to conference, the Black woman lawyer was always left behind. On one day, she physically displayed her frustration, her body language agitated and taut, and mumbled to herself that the next time she was going to go back there with the two White male lawyers.

When the jury selection pool of thirteen entered, everyone was White, apart from one Asian woman and one Latinx man—not a single Black person among them. We found this maddening and patently racist given that so many Black people worked in this municipal building and otherwise passed through it daily. There are Black communities scattered throughout the Twin Cities. But here we were, a Black woman and a Black man from ultra-diverse New York City, being sued, in a majority White city and a majority White state, by a White woman represented by two lead White male lawyers, with a White woman judge overseeing this trial of what would eventually be a jury of five White women, one White man, and one Asian woman, there to determine whether or not we, a Black woman and a Black man from New York, would pay April Sellers, a White woman, hundreds of thousands of dollars for an email alleged to be defamatory and hurtful to her career in the Twin Cities of Minnesota. We now understood why so many Black Minnesotans warned Jinah and me throughout 2018 about a phenomenon called "Minnesota nice." In other words, the state pays lip service to diversity, to inclusion. Folks openly celebrate global Black pop icon Prince as a native son and give group bear hugs to legendary Minnesota Black athletes like Kirby Puckett, Kevin

Garnett, and Adrian Peterson. But one prominent Black resident of the state told us not to be fooled by these public displays and that racism was as bad, if not worse, in Minnesota than in Mississippi. No matter where we go, some White folks want our music, our culture, our cool, our votes, our sports brilliance, and our bodies for certain pleasures or curiosities, but it seems the totality of our beings counts for little.

We heard that the trial would last three days, Wednesday through Friday. From the very beginning, once the jury was seated and given its instructions and the trial commenced, April Sellers cried constantly. Her lead attorney Aaron Scott also cried at the start of the trial, as if on cue, and portrayed a case of mistaken identity as worthy of a whopping financial settlement as opposed to a simple retraction and a public apology. He offered his minimal research on me at the beginning: that I was a cast member on the first season of MTV's *The Real World*; that I was a "famous writer," a "celebrity author," with major publication credits; and that I travel the country and the world delivering speeches. I am not a celebrity at all, merely a public figure because of my work as a writer, speaker, and activist for over thirty years, who sometimes appears on national television to offer my perspective on the significant issues of our times. Aaron Scott, a lawyer in a medium-sized city in Middle America, wanted to convince the jury that my status makes me a celebrity with a limitless supply of cash. Aaron Scott demonstrated his cluelessness about the nature of celebrity. Folks who live in a bubble do not understand the detrimental nature of America's obsession with celebrity. Lawsuits like this happen when people think they know someone about whom they really know nothing. Anyone can Google me to find out who I am and what I do. If I were, say, a college student, or someone who just had a regular everyday job, or worked in a factory, or was a street sweeper, or a homeless man, there would be no lawsuit. If it were only my wife—the artist and educator—there would be no lawsuit. If Aaron Scott asked any of the many writers who live in the Twin Cities, he would get an earful about the financial challenges associated with a writer's life. He would have learned that most writers do not make enough money to sustain themselves... particularly those who write books like mine. I did not spend years writing for film or television. Not one of my previous 13 books made it to *The New York Times Best Seller List*, or any bestseller list. Activists like me do not hold jobs with benefits at a not-for-profit that provides us with regular revenue streams. I work strictly for myself, am self-employed. I am one of those kinds of activists, one who has mostly worked for free on causes I believe in my entire adult life, from the anti-apartheid movement to cases of racial profiling and police brutality, to relief help after both 9/11 and Hurricane Katrina, to the annual clothing drive I run for homeless young people in New York City every

December, for the past 20 years. Activists like me do this work because it is our life's work—our passion—to serve others, because we care, because we love empowering others. Even with my wife's theater production, *SHE*, I never received a salary as the main producer. Moreover, after I sent the letter to April Sellers and BCCed it to 35 or so people in Minnesota, I let it go, never sent it anywhere else, never posted it anywhere else, nothing. I wanted to protect and to defend my wife. In the past, I have responded to plenty of crazy, attack-mode emails and social media posts, but no one threatened to sue me. As the victim of so many public attacks on television, on the radio, on social media, in newspapers and magazines, I do not want to engage in a sustained campaign against anyone. Just not who I am as a human being, and just not something I have the time and energy to do. As I listened to Aaron Scott's opening statement, which included the kind of coded language historically used to paint a negative picture of Black males, I reflected on the long history of White men doing this to Black men, to Black people of every gender identity, be it a White segregationist in the Old South or a Fox News commentator in this 21st century. When that happens, some White liberals unwittingly become allies—bedfellows—to White conservatives and put forth the same stereotypes as those White conservatives. Aaron Scott acted as if I were guilty of a far more terrible offense than sending an email to the wrong person. It did not matter that once we saw an affidavit for a different April Sellers, of Ohio, in June 2018, we offered to apologize. And like I said we repeated that offer several times leading up to the trial. It did not matter that Judge Karen Janisch, in a moment of empathy for Jinah and me weeks before the trial, said to Aaron Scott, with our lawyer Lee Hutton present, "Why can't you accept an apology?" He saw me—and this lawsuit—as a path to make a name for himself and April Sellers, the plaintiff, played a minor role in that scenario. This was really *The Aaron Scott Show*, the entire trial. American history and American realities be damned if he would allow a little thing, like what appeared to my wife and me as a grossly personal attack, to deter him from his date with destiny. I smiled to myself as Aaron Scott gave his opening statement lambasting me and my character, while not saying much of anything about my wife. I thought back to the June 2018 deposition in New York City and how, during one of the breaks, Aaron Scott made it clear he was a Democrat and seemed absolutely disgusted by one Donald Trump. A White liberal, which is very different from being a White progressive, professes to be immune from racism, from hate. Yet some White liberals want the same access to the levers of power and of privilege as White conservatives. True White progressives understand that if White Americans are serious about change, are serious about ending racism, then you do not practice or embrace racism, White supremacy, White privilege, against Black people or people of color in any form, including using the legal system to hurt or take them down when they are essentially good people, as Jinah and I are, when they clearly did nothing–nothing–that warrants such treatment. Again, we were on trial for an email. For an email....

The nine Scottsboro Boys–accused in the 1930s in Alabama, by two White women, of rape–went to prison, their lives forever destroyed. Most of them died tragically young, even in the face of evidence exonerating them. Emmett Till–a 14-year-old Black boy from Chicago–traveled to Money, Mississippi, to visit his family during the summer of 1955. Till was accused of whistling at a White woman, and a group of White men decided to teach this "Uppity N****r" a lesson, using the colossal weight of White supremacy and their White male privilege to take his young life. The Central Park Five– arrested for the rape of a White woman jogger in New York City in 1989–spent their formative years in prison after sham trials that resulted in long prison sentences. Thirty years and a multimillion-dollar settlement later, and despite total exoneration, they still live under the crushing burdens of mental and spiritual terrorism over their lost years. When White men or White women do not take it upon themselves to think about the daily and harsh reality of racism in America, when they do not feel love... only hate, no peace, only rage and war, no understanding, only a bloodthirst for revenge, you will beat Emmett Till unconscious, you will smash his brain, gouge his eyes out, tie a fan around his neck, and drown him, too, to make sure he is dead. Or you will use the court room—the legal system—as your noose, as your rifle, your words against an accused Black person your executioner's song. And when some White liberals or racist White conservatives hear Black folks or other folks of color even utter the word "racism," they say things like "This has nothing to do with race" or "Here they go again playing the race card" or "I am not racist" or "That history stuff you keep bringing up is in the past, let it go...." They will say and do anything to deny and deflect what we know to be systemic racism and continue to wreak havoc on society's most vulnerable—expecting us to ignore the truth we see around us every day... the sheer insanity and heartlessness of racism, the denial of freedom and of equality, the absence of rational thought—replaced by emotional and spiritual warfare—

I likewise wondered, as I listened to Aaron Scott's opening statement, why he insisted on bringing up MTV's *The Real World* repeatedly—a show that I appeared on in 1992, almost three decades ago. But then it dawned on me: a lot of White males of my generation—Generation X—across the United States, have hated me since my participation in that reality show because I called Becky, one of my White woman castmates, the "b-word" and called the other White woman castmate, Julie, "racist," and got into heated arguments with them both... in living color. I acted like the person I was at that time: a young Black male in America trying to figure this world out, sometimes mad clear and sometimes mad confused. I did not bite my tongue when I had something to say. Do I regret saying those things and wish I had made my points in a different way? Yes, absolutely. But like most young people, I evolved and grew over the ensuing years. Some folks choose to ignore that because they prefer to define you... attempting to tell you who you are and put you in a box of their own design, like forever. It never dawned on me until after my experience on the inaugural season of *The Real World* what a big deal it was for a Black man to interact with White women as I did. My first realization came when my mother called me in abject fear after watching one of the episodes. She yelled at me and told me that I should never speak to a White woman like that ever again. My actions gave her nightmarish flashbacks to her childhood and young adulthood in the Low Country of South Carolina and the bucketful of stories of what could—and did—happen to any Black person, usually a Black male, who dared to say anything that could be construed as disrespectful to anyone in the White community—and God forbid if that Black male was accused of injuring a White woman. Those who allegedly violated those established racial boundaries found themselves with a one-way ticket to the nearest high tree with a rope around their neck and a celebration, including local media with cameras and men, women, and children reveling with enthusiasm rivaling a modern-day Super Bowl or March Madness. Yes, I thought of those White males—especially many straight ones—who label me in person, on social media, and in emails as they often do to other Black males who speak their truth. Yes, I have encountered men like Aaron Scott across America, who judge by the images of me the producers chose to use on *The Real World*. Ironically, the two White women from the show, Julie and Becky, remain close to me these nearly thirty years later. We love each other and, indeed, consider ourselves family, because of that unique experience we seven castmates shared. No matter, when there is an agenda someone like me is religiously transformed from an activist with a national and international reputation for integrity into a liar and a career killer. Many White people in America see Black people through a twisted lens as morally bankrupt characters who cannot be trusted or believed. They manufacture scenarios to derail any attempt to establish the truth.

Hit pause: At this point, I need to scratch and burn the dead skin from my soul and ask myself a few humble questions: How do I avoid putting myself in the crosshairs of spiritual and mental and physical warfare as a Black person in America? Should I ignore hate-filled emails like the one that led to the lawsuit against Jinah and me, should I pretend no one has told me to go back to Africa, that no one is cursing or name-calling me, my momma, my family, my people, as easily as they brush their teeth or sip their morning coffee? Where can I, we, go to be safe, to be careful, while still being true to ourselves and our moral and historical and political obligation to confront those who would do harm to us, because we are Colored-Negro-Black-African? Or was Tupac Shakur right and prophetic in one of the many interviews I did with him, that there is no place called careful? I mean....

As his first witness, Aaron Scott called the Ohio woman named April Sellers who signed the affidavit in June 2018, saying that she did, in fact, send my wife the racist and sexist email in October of 2017. To the surprise of our lawyer, myself, my wife, and Maddy Buxton, a Black woman walked in carrying five of my thirteen books under her right arm. Tall and slim, she had a flower pinned on the left side of her hair as if she were jazz singer Billie Holiday. From the moment she began speaking, we knew something was not quite right. The Black April Sellers, as we came to call her privately, said she was a huge fan and admirer of my work, praised my writings, said she read much of what I had written, and claimed to be a journalist who had interviewed iconic figures like former First Lady Barbara Bush (no record of this interview appears when searching extensively online for "April Sellers" and "First Lady Barbara Bush"). The Black April Sellers also said she lived just outside of Cleveland, had gone to historically Black Howard University, and came to Minneapolis to right the wrong that had been done to the other April Sellers. She recalled my appearance on *The Oprah Winfrey Show* in 2009, when I talked about ending violence against women and girls unaware that I pushed a girlfriend into a bathroom door in 1991. That gave her the impetus to read some of my work in depth and became concerned that I would physically violate a woman again. I did not... not in any fashion. No matter, the Black April Sellers said she became concerned for my wife's safety and felt compelled to send that email warning my wife of possible dangers.

As I sat there listening to the Black April Sellers, I could not help but think back to the 1990 film *Misery*, based on the Stephen King novel of the same name. I never read the book, but the movie version terrified me as a young writer because it centered on an obsessed fan who stalked, harassed, kidnapped, and tortured an author. Here I sat in a courtroom a few feet from a human being who mixed my life and life work with fiction. Indeed, I sat in the courtroom listening to a human being who praised me while she quoted passages that I wrote many years back to justify sending that hate-filled email to Jinah in the first place. And during cross-examination from our lawyer the Black April Sellers stated that Aaron Scott's law firm paid her travel expenses from Ohio, including her hotel bill, and that Aaron Scott furnished her with his questions in advance of the trial. She also stated during cross-examination that she started communicating with Aaron Scott in January of 2018, when he filed the lawsuit against my wife and me, although a signed affidavit did not come until June of 2018. This was all recorded by the court reporter, the transcript of which can be obtained by anyone. When the Black April Sellers completed her testimony, she rose slowly, smiled nervously, gathered the five books I authored under her right arm, quick-stepped off the witness stand, paused briefly at the table where Aaron Scott sat, then kept walking right out of the courtroom... gone, forever. I found it preposterous that the Black April Sellers became the star witness and ally for the White April Sellers who had filed suit against my wife and me for somewhere between $500,000 and $1,000,000.

But so it was—

(The ironic footnote to the testimony of the Black April Sellers is that about 9 months later my wife and I both received letter notices that she had filed for bankruptcy. Was this to protect herself from a potential lawsuit from us? We do not know, but the timing was very strange....)

When the White April Sellers took the stand, she continued the crying that began the moment she entered the courtroom. I sat there listening to her testimony and again I knew—as Black people with a White judge and a majority White jury always know—that we did not stand a chance, that the trial should have ended immediately and a verdict announced, given that we could not pay whatever dollar amount the jury was going to award her anyway. But instead we sat there and listened to April Sellers talk–without proof– about how we ruined her life and career in 2018. We sat there and listened to April Sellers say–without convincing proof– that two Minnesota foundations rejected her applications for funding based on the open letter that we sent to her. We sat there and listened to April Sellers say–without convincing proof–that she did not leave her home to go to public events in the Minneapolis-St. Paul area in fear of the way she would be treated because of our open letter. Her attorney offered no evidence that anyone who received the open letter felt any differently about her, or that that they even read it, for that matter. April Sellers and her lawyer made the argument that this open letter, which my wife and I–who live in New York City–mistakenly sent to the wrong April Sellers, erased her self-proclaimed 20 years of professional work in Minnesota. During cross examination by our attorney Lee Hutton, April Sellers, who testified that she owned and ran her dance company–April Sellers Dance Collective–could not say how much she paid her dancers, how much money she earned prior to this lawsuit, provided minimal financial details of her own efforts in spite of her claim that she worked in various spaces, as an artist, as an educator, for the past 20 years. She could not testify regarding the not-for-profit status of her company, or even if she or her company paid taxes of any kind, or how and who received monies for her work, be it her company or her as individual. All of this can be found in the transcript of the trial. During Lee Hutton's questioning, the White April Sellers fell completely apart, because neither she nor her attorney presented any evidence that our email destroyed her life or her career. I reiterate that all of this can be verified by reading the public transcript of the trial. Jinah and I, on the other hand, can answer questions about the details of our work on *SHE*, including all our funding sources, our payments to every dancer, actor, and other employees, and every expenditure for other purposes.

But please let me also be clear. As I listened to April Sellers, I felt waves of empathy and compassion for her. Just like April Sellers has no clue what it is to be a Black person falsely accused of something, I have no idea what it is to be a woman falsely accused of something. I wish I had never sent the email in the first place and I take full responsibility for that, for the grief it brought to April Sellers in Minnesota, to my wife, to me. In the quieter moments I have even asked myself what possessed me to respond to whoever April Sellers was that sent that email to Jinah. What was happening inside of me that compelled me to say something, to do something, then and there, when I have ignored so many similar types of slings and arrows in the past? Was it because I was a man, and despite my proclamations to the contrary, I still, somewhere in my woke-ness, believe that men should defend women no matter what? Was it because April Sellers was a woman and I felt the need to put her in her place, as a man, because somehow and somewhere her email struck a very serious nerve with me, made me feel fragile, vulnerable, and I had to push back, not just to defend my wife but also, alas, my manhood? I wish I, we, had responded to April Sellers when she emailed and asked us to call her, not once, but twice; I wish there was a safe space where I could have reconciled the matter and apologized before it spun so quickly and so wildly out of control, taking us all through the torment of a lawsuit and a trial. I wish I could have spoken with April Sellers during that trial and talked, human to human, about what we had in common, about the shared suffering many of us experience in this world. Yes, hurt people hurt other people... And no one should ever be falsely accused of anything. God knows I know.

However, what April Sellers, and her lawyer, failed to grasp as we sat there listening to them disparage me repeatedly, is that by hammering at me, at my character, at my very being, they did the same thing to me that they accused my wife and I of doing with the open letter. When April Sellers said in one journal entry, read aloud in court, that this "is my #MeToo moment" and added right after, that she felt "raped," she had plunged herself into the muddy waters of coded language and age-old stereotypes. Nobody was raped or physically assaulted in any way, not even close. Why use a word like that to describe an email mistakenly sent to the wrong person and blind copied to thirty-something people, none of whom even responded to it? I knew, again, that with a jury consisting of mostly White women in Minnesota—a state deemed to be one of the most uncomfortable in the United States for Black folks to live—that we faced certain defeat in this case. I slumped in my chair in that courtroom and my mind filled with thoughts of how racism in these United States goes beyond being a physical crime against the bodies of Black people and other people of color. Worse, it is an emotional and spiritual crime... an attack on our minds and our souls. Most White Americans do not comprehend how thoroughly this disease called racism corrupts. This deadly plague is contracted from families, from schools, from religious institutions, from friends and colleagues and co-workers, from the mass media culture, it exists here there everywhere. Read any of my 13 books, listen to any of my speeches or interviews. I make it clear that I come from horrific poverty... raised by a single mother... only saw my father the first eight years of my life on two or three occasions... my mother, because she had been damaged, damaged me physically, mentally, verbally... violence all about me in my 'hood in my hometown... angry and violent toward males and females as a child into my adult years... pushed a girlfriend into a bathroom door in July 1991. I own all of it... just like I own that I have spent years and years in therapy...

done years and years of spiritual work... became an ally to women and girls from those very same 1990s to the present... strive to re-think and to re-define manhood constantly. I do this work in diverse communities, at high schools and grade schools, on college campuses, in corporate America, at prisons, with speeches, workshops, training sessions. Aaron Scott went out of his way to take the true arc of my journey out of context–to reduce me–as that hate-filled email sent to Jinah did–to a monster. In short, the open letter to April Sellers was mistakenly sent to the wrong person, something I said I regretted when I was on the stand myself at the trial. But that did not matter. This came down to a legal lynching, a mob mentality, to get money. The plaintiff, led by her attorney, used anything and everything they could to sway the majority White jury to rule against me, against us.

And that effort included bringing Rohan Preston, my fellow writer, my fellow journalist, to testify against me under subpoena. I knew this was problematic the morning of his testimony because I saw him outside the courtroom laughing and chatting with April Sellers–a man I have known for 25 years–who texted me a couple of weeks before the trial and claimed that I had misrepresented him in my deposition (Aaron Scott had passed along my deposition to Rohan Preston). A man whose work and opinions I had valued, and, because of that, I believed him that October 2017 day while I rode in an Uber in Brooklyn with my wife. Yes, his words led me to write and email the open letter in the first place. Yet, he testified under oath that he had said nothing of the sort and praised April Sellers as an outstanding artist and outstanding citizen and questioned my journalistic integrity. Yes, on the stand, without provocation from either Aaron Scott or Lee Hutton, Rohan Preston referred to the open letter sent to April Sellers as a "career killer" without offering any proof backing up that description. This is all in the transcript of the trial. I felt duped, monumentally betrayed and backstabbed by Rohan Preston, and my entire being felt as if it would fall apart—

When it came time for the closing arguments, I listened to our lawyer, Lee Hutton, brilliantly break down why the entire lawsuit was a sham. He was prepared, he was organized, he was articulate, he was dynamic—one of the best lawyers I've met anywhere in the country. He poked holes in Aaron Scott's arguments. He exposed, as he did during his cross-examination of April Sellers, that the plaintiff and her attorney presented no evidence of any financial damage that she suffered as a result of our email. He reminded the jury that during the cross-examination of April Sellers, she could not answer basic questions about how much she paid folks who worked with her or the inner financial workings of her own company. He told the jury that this lawsuit was about money, "a come up" as Black folks say—an on-the-spot winning lottery ticket for her. He told the jury that the plaintiff's case was a mirage to make it appear that we launched a concerted, calculated, and ongoing attack on April Sellers, when that was not the case at all. He told the jury to ignore the theatrics and the high drama and see the case for what it was: an email sent to the wrong person.

When Aaron Scott got up to give his closing argument, I stuck two plugs into my ears and pressed my fingers into them, pushing them as far in as I could. Thus, I did not hear a single word he said because I did not want to. I endured enough ugliness and attacks in the past year, since Aaron Scott first sent the email in December of 2017 telling Jinah and I we were being sued. To me, it was verbal and emotional abuse and there is but so much a person can take. The trial dragged on, unnecessarily, as Aaron Scott repeated the same arguments interminably, put forth the same "evidence" interminably, asked the same questions interminably, to the point where we requested that my wife be allowed to return home to New York City for fear of losing her job as a part-time teacher. And there I remained, in Minnesota, past those first three days, through the weekend, into a new week, for seven full days. But for the kindness of a few old, and new, friends in the Twin Cities, I truly believe that I would have suffered a nervous breakdown during my time there, particularly after my wife departed. I began my own healing process then and there, with the plugs in my ears. When Aaron Scott was finished with his closing argument, I took the earplugs out... at peace with whatever decision the jury might render. As artists, activists, advocates for social justice causes, and educators, my wife and I do not have an abundance of money. From our perspective, this trial centered on a White woman versus two Black people; an artist and educator versus two artists, two educators; a person with no money versus two people with no money; a self-proclaimed social justice advocate versus two acknowledged social justice warriors. It was classic divide and conquer. Throughout my life as a leader in America I have engaged in conflict resolution with people from all walks of life. I never experienced anything like this trial on such a personal level. It came to represent, in microcosm, the current state in America. Some White people feel emboldened, because of the conscious and subconscious and toxic nature of racism in the era of Donald Trump, to come after Black people, to come after people of color. Life should not be this hard. It numbs the mind to consider what we people who live on the margins deal with daily in this place called America. Indeed, I thought often, during the trial, of that old joke in Black American activist circles: that the only difference between certain kinds of White liberals and a racist White conservative is that that those certain kinds of White liberals will just hang you, the Black person, from a lower tree.

I did not attend the verdict because I knew what it would be and could not bear to hear it. Plus, it was mad obvious the jury did not want to be there, was disgusted that this trial had dragged on day to day, and the one White male juror visibly and aggressively flashed his fatigue and outrage whenever the judge said we were heading to another day. The jury deliberated for maybe an hour or two, if that. We lost. The jury awarded April Sellers $220,000. As our attorney said, April Sellers' lawyer never seems to have checked our incomes... our debt... anything, before filing the lawsuit. He did not subpoena any of our financial records during this process. He relied on the ridiculous assumption that because of my status as a public figure, I accumulated great wealth... when nothing could be farther from the truth. In that context, the lawsuit, the depositions, the mediation, the trial—everything—constituted a colossal waste of time, money, energy, and emotions on both sides; and this will be dragged out with appeals and legal maneuverings that could take years. The entire experience hurt my wife and me, and we know that hurt people hurt other people. The original email from the Black April Sellers hurt us, and we responded in a hurtful manner. Our email hurt the White April Sellers, and she responded. A lawsuit came less than a month later including ridiculous and false accusations about me. "This is America," as Childish Gambino famously rapped in that song. Indeed, it is. Hurt people hurt other people, and we live in an acutely traumatized nation. That means all of us—we the people—hurt each other here there everywhere—on social media, with emails, at work, at home, in our families, in our communities, with lawsuits, with mass shootings, and more, and more, and more. *Hurt people hurt other people....*

Jinah and I do not hate anyone and will not be drawn to that mindset despite how we feel about this Minnesota madness. That is not who we are. I love people, all people, and forever will, even when I feel profoundly saddened and betrayed by people, any people. I choose love, Jinah and I choose love. It bears repeating that as we suffered through the absurdities and indignities of this trial, White and Black Minnesotans stepped up and supported us, cared for us, loved on us, because they knew, including some who attended the trial, how insufferable this was for us. We reminded ourselves over and over that we are good people, individually and as a married couple. We seek freedom, justice, and equality for all people, and that truly means all people. We know that love is the revolution, the only answer, to heal, save, and change America, to heal, save, and change this world. But we can never love others, never heal others, if we do not heal ourselves, if we do not know and love ourselves. That lesson became clear in the month following the trial when the two major Minneapolis-St. Paul newspapers—*The Star Tribune and City Pages*—published feature articles highlighting the lawsuit and judgement, strictly from the perspective of April Sellers and Aaron Scott. The pieces written by journalists David Chanen of *The Star Tribune* and Susan Du of *City Pages* followed the narrative begun by Aaron Scott. We found it particularly disappointing that Susan Du, an Asian American, did not see our case in its essence: a manipulation of the legal system and of local media to paint one-dimensional pictures of people of color. I agree with nothing, like nothing, that Donald Trump stands for, but I do see a significant amount of "fake news" out here. I say that because I have witnessed it as a journalist and on the other side as the subject of media distortions. For that reason, we chose not to respond to either publication's inquiry for an interview because of how traumatized we were by the entire Minnesota saga, and because I wanted to do an interview where I could provide a chronology of the events from our perspective. I did that with the Black weekly paper, the *Minnesota Spokesman-Recorder*, because I needed a space where I also felt safe—a space where I could tell my whole truth, not fragments of the truth, and refute the mischaracterizations reported in the accounts of the trial presented in the two mainstream newspapers. The same company owns *The Star Tribune* and *City Pages*, and, as I mentioned earlier, one of *The Star Tribune*'s writers, Rohan Preston, testified against my wife and me at the trial. That notwithstanding, and as I said, both publications printed lopsided articles about the trial. As a trained journalist who has been in the media profession since the mid-1980s, and who has written for newspapers, magazines, websites, and also produced content for television, documentary films, and podcasts, I always scan every single space I am in very closely, to see who is there, and I always pay attention to every single detail in that space. The courtroom, during our seven-day trial, was mostly empty except for a few supporters of both sides now and again. I knew what David Chanen of *The Star Tribune* and Susan Du of *City Pages* looked like, I knew who they were because whenever I am in any city, I always read the local papers, and neither was there for more than a day or two of the seven-day trial. Yet both penned articles about the matter as if they had been present every single day, as if they had done fair and balanced research and investigation about the entire matter, from all angles. They had not, as evidenced by their respective articles. It was drive-by journalism with sensationalistic, click-bait headlines: "A Facebook post called Minneapolis dancer a racist. They had the wrong April Sellers," *The Star Tribune*, David Chanen, January 29, 2019; "The Smear: A career-killing lie almost ruined this rising Minneapolis dance star," *City Pages*, Susan Du, January 23, 2019. Ms. Du's article even dissed and mocked me for how I dressed: "He exudes an aristocratic defiance, wearing a prim navy suit, pocket square, and cashmere scarf wrapped tight like an ascot." If Ms. Du had actually been paying closer attention, and if she had actually been there the entire trial, she would have noticed, one, that I do not own a navy blue suit, just a navy blue jacket that I wore several times with two different colored pants during those long seven days because, in fact, I barely own any suits at all; that my scarf was actually cotton, not cashmere, and very cheap, and I wore it because it was December in Minnesota and freezing outside, and also mad cold inside that courtroom daily, and because I was coughing and sick for a good portion of the trial. But, again, these are the kinds of inaccurate things often written about Black people, about people of color, in our times, and historically, to suggest that something is wrong with us, to imply someone is an "Uppity N****r" just by the way they are dressed, does a great disservice to the diversity and humanity of Black people, to the diversity and humanity of people of color. We are rarely seen as whole human beings, and our side of the story rarely matters. For sure, the folks at *The Star Tribune* and *City Pages* failed to realize that by publishing those articles they fanned the flames of a dispute that should have ended with the judgment in favor of April Sellers in December 2018. As a direct result of those two articles, Jinah and I became the victims of a merciless pursuit and harassment by hateful people, hateful White people, who attacked us via email, on Facebook, on Instagram, on Twitter.

Yes, those two articles unleashed a fury of racist trolls who called me mean-spirited names like "rapist" on social media. Let me be clear: I never raped anyone nor has anyone ever accused me of rape. The racist trolls seemed to be mostly offended that I did not offer an apology, ever, to the White

April Sellers, which, again, is patently false. The racist trolls repeatedly said that nothing that happened to us involved race or racism in this nation. They wanted to deny us—or any African American—the basic human right to draw upon our individual and collective experiences as they relate to our nation's sordid history and present-day realities. In their eyes, we could not say that something just ain't right with any of this. We simply want to be—as the Black mental-health expert and scholar Ed Garnes says on the regular—our whole and authentic selves. I say, additionally, that we just want to be free, to express what we feel, who we are, without fear of being inhumanely punished for that expression. The racist trolls—mostly White males—express themselves freely and aggressively with their rage—so much so that they even bombarded the GoFundMe page I set up during the trial so that we could simply pay the mounting legal fees created by this entire affair. When attorney Aaron Scott got wind of the GoFundMe page, he sent an angry note to our lawyer, Lee Hutton, taking issue with statements I had made in my GoFundMe page, and highlighting for Lee the criminal liability I could be exposed to under Minnesota law, including jail. Aaron Scott is a lawyer, not the police, not a judge, a lawyer. I wonder if his law firm, Fox Rothschild, would ever allow a Black attorney—regardless of gender identity—to doggedly pursue, with cold-blooded efficiency and thousands upon thousands of wasted dollars, a frivolous lawsuit over an email mistakenly sent to the wrong person? I wonder if Fox Rothschild grasps the devastating emotional and financial toll that legal action wrought on us... our marriage... our love... our truth... our faith and trust in each other?

My wife and I want what all people want: to feel safe and free. You don't want to be constantly looking over your shoulder wondering who will be the next to assault you—verbally, physically, or emotionally. Politicians like the current occupant of the White House will come and go, while many of us in America will never be truly free... including Aaron Scott and April Sellers. Ms. Sellers accepted the narrative that Jinah Parker and I are bad people who intentionally sought to destroy her. She internalized that fiction and became its prisoner: believing that the financial security that she never found through her professional life would come to her through this judgment. As a fellow artist, I ponder a larger issue. Why do we live in a nation where 1% hold most of the wealth and power, while those of us who dedicate our lives to higher ideals like justice and fair play and the arts barely scrape by? This Minnesota lawsuit reminded me a lot of when I lived in Newark, New Jersey, in another chapter of my life, far, far ago, and how poor people, Black, Latinx, Portuguese, all would try to "catch cases," as we called it, by getting hit by a city bus, or falling down on an uneven sidewalk, anything, they hoped, that would lead to a life-changing payday. But what kind of empowerment and freedom does that represent when someone resorts to lying or stepping over others to achieve some measure of success? Or, when a human being builds their personhood on such a flimsy foundation as ego, competition, and winning at all costs, we see the true nature of depravity in our America. The struggle is living in a diseased culture that beats many of us down, regardless of our race, culture, creed, identities, because that is what diseased cultures do. Jinah and I suffer post-traumatic stress disorder (PTSD) from the ongoing injustices associated with the trial and its aftermath. Our marriage, our bond, our trust in each other, in large part because of Minnesota, has been profoundly disturbed. Yet we continue to preach and to practice love, hard as it may be and despite what we have had to endure, because of an email mistakenly sent to the wrong person—

DREAM #4

Yes, I know how it feels to be broken, and sorrowful, and defeated, and angry, because of what I have experienced. But I cannot and will not sit there, stay there, because whenever the depression, the sadness, become completely agonizing— and it has been, over and over—I think about my ancestors, what they survived, the pathological viciousness of the Middle

Passage, of slavery, of segregation, of auction blocks and whips and nooses and axe-chopped private parts and water hoses and tear gas and rocks and barking dogs and voter suppression—I cannot and will not give up, I cannot and will not lose faith in the human spirit, in human beings, in what is possible, in spite of the slings and arrows. Moreover, I understand the difference between proactive anger and reactionary anger. We use proactive anger to build and create things that challenge injustice, fear, division, violence, hate. When we resort to reactionary anger, we embrace fear, division, violence, hate, and become bridge-destroyers instead of bridge-builders. Proactive anger frees us, while reactionary anger locks us in a pitch-black spiritual and emotional prison, fighting ourselves, fighting each other. Let me be clear: I want to be free. But I must confess that in recent years, I reverted to anger, to that pitch-black prison I had not visited in many years, because I am traumatized, so pathetically traumatized. Because of things like the Brooklyn police arrest and the Minnesota lawsuit. Because of things like the constant racial profiling videos and racial murders of Black folks plastered across news outlets and social media. Because of one mass shooting after another—here there everywhere—with no ending to gun violence even remotely in sight. Because of immigrant families being separated and locked up the way my ancestors—as kidnapped African slaves —were separated and locked up. Because of the sheer ridiculousness of Donald Trump and his daily antics, which bring to mind an unrepentant and clueless abuser battering his wife and children relentlessly. Because of the obnoxious and brazen displays of White supremacy and White supremacist symbols in our fair land—be it the Confederate flag, or Confederate statues, or instances of Blackface, or sports teams refusing to change racist sports names and logos. Because of the tiresome money woes that eat, day by day, at bits of your sanity, bits of your humanity, making you feel worthless even as you work yourself into total exhaustion. Because of the horrors I re-live daily/weekly/monthly while working on my next book, the long-overdue biography of Tupac Shakur, and not only having to carry around the ordeals of my own life, but also his, his mother's, his family's, the communities that shaped him, hearing, from multiple sources, how Tupac was pumped with bullets on that fateful Las Vegas night, how he died, slowly, in that hospital room, how he himself lived in tremendous turmoil those very short 25 years, to the point where I have had to pause... to take breaks... to gasp... to vomit tears, just to keep going with the book—and to not go totally insane while working on this Tupac biography. Because of my mother and her illnesses, which forces me, an only child, to be her sole caretaker, and to sit and absorb anew her past, her verbal and emotional atomic bombs, her sword-wielding demons, which I have also wielded at various points in my own life. My mother continues to wrestle with her health, yes, but, as difficult as it is to say publicly, her emotional being is even more fragile. She has been damaged from birth because of what America, and her hometown, and her community, and her family, and my father, and her employers, did to her. There was no Oprah for my mother, no sister circles, no therapy or women's retreats. There was no yoga or meditation... and there certainly is no love or hugs for women like her. She stitched the frayed fabric of her life together and made a way out of no way, as she, a poor single mother, raised me. Only because of miracles do we both still exist, but exist we do... dancing with my mother and my mother dancing with me, hurt people hurting people, an endless cycle of insults and wounds that we inflict upon others. I know this and I ache thinking of how we assault and brutalize our children, how we assault and brutalize our young people, without ever realizing it. Although I did not comprehend it initially, as America has rapidly deteriorated in this era of Trump, so did I. I know this because what happened to me in Brooklyn and in Minnesota reflects the current state of our country. We are a lost people. And while I continue to believe in things like voting, in paying attention to current events, to the general importance of elections, I also know, in the pit of my gut, that whether liberal or conservative, Democrat or Republican, blue state or red state, Donald Trump or Barack Obama or someone else, even the occupant of the Oval Office will not matter, in the grand scheme of things, if we do not get the soul of this nation right... once and for all. The burning truth is that the system is the problem and, as I said, this is a diseased culture that so many of us embrace fanatically, obsessively, religiously. Some of us say "Make America Great Again," practicing a kind of enthusiastic ignorance that disregards the American past—riddled with hate and violence and genocide and slavery and a thoughtless disregard for practically everyone at some point, whether we be Native Americans, or Black, or immigrants of any background, or Jewish, or Muslim, or LBGTQ+, or disabled, or poor, or people with dwarfism, or women of any race or color, or young, or an elder. Democracy that does not apply to all people all the time is not Democracy. Those working-class White folks, in the South, in the North, in the Midwest, on the West Coast, who faithfully support what the Republican Party has become—from Ronald Reagan to Donald Trump—are people I cross paths within my travels around America as a public speaker. I believe in the essential goodness of people. But when society brainwashes you into believing in White supremacy, in White superiority, in us versus them, that God is White and is only White, that this country somehow magically appeared without the very serious oppression of Native Americans and Africans turned into slaves and free labor, then you will also believe that there was once a time when America was great... for you. And that is a lie. Since its founding, certain kinds of wealthy White men with power have controlled our country. Change has only come when marginalized groups demanded it. Imagine if there had been no abolitionist or anti-slavery movement; imagine if there had been no labor movement; imagine if there had been no anti-lynching movement; imagine if there had been no women's movement; imagine if there had been no Civil Rights Movement; imagine if there had been no Stonewall or gay rights movement; imagine if there had been no anti-nuclear or environmental movements; imagine if organizations like The Innocence Project did not exist to help free the wrongly accused from years in prison; imagine life without Black Lives Matter and the #MeToo movement. Imagine what America would be like if the majestic Fannie Lou Hamer had not said "I am sick and tired of bein' sick and tired." Presidential and other political elections come and go, but at root is the issue of power, who holds it and who does not. Until we address that primal conflict in our America, the needle will not move in a sustained and life-transforming way for we the people. We will forever chase our tails, engaging in the same conversations and doing the same things again and again, expecting a different result... Albert Einstein's very definition of insanity—

So, when some White folks were utterly shocked, frightened, when Donald Trump became president, and expected, say, African Americans to be as horrified as they were and are about the Trump presidency, about Trumpville, to co-sign that these are in fact the worst of times, our collective sorrow songs chanted back to them: Where have you been since 1619, what have you not been hearing/seeing/feeling that we have been hearing/seeing/feeling all along? I guess you never knew that most of the first 17 American presidents owned slaves; that presidents 15 through 35, including Abe Lincoln and John Kennedy, presided over a land that had slavery or continued the legacy of slavery with vicious and inhumane legal and illegal segregation; that while president 36, Lyndon Johnson, did push through the Civil Rights Act and the Voting Rights Bill in the 1960s because of a people's feet a-marching, by the time we got to president number 40, Ronald Reagan, these very minimal civil rights victories were already being eroded or outright eliminated. I guess you never heard of sharecropping; or burning and bombing of entire communities like the African American Greenwood section of Tulsa, Oklahoma, the "Black Wall Street." I guess you never knew of strange fruits dressed as human beings dangling from trees, or drug epidemics like crack devastating whole families and whole communities? I guess you've never heard of the prison-industrial complex, or Hurricane Katrina, or Trayvon Martin or Sandra Bland, either? And, so, here we are at Donald Trump, president 45, and you want us to say these are the worst of times. That means you must've never felt—in your bones, in your pores—the aching depths of our music, our Internet before there was Internet: our field hollers... our spirituals... our ragtime... our jazz... our blues... our rock 'n' roll... our soul... our funk... our hip-hop. You did not hear a people singing of pain and bewilderment long ago—in our churches big and small—the ones with White Jesus, the ones with Black Jesus, the ones with no Jesus, gritting our gums and bearing down on that cross, as we applied prayer clothes and prayer oils and hooted and hollered to the Lord—falling down, falling out, running laps, shooting snot from our noses and sweat from our temples, leaping for joy, leaping for our savior, leaping for a savior, anyone and anything that will set us free?

We must stop saying America is a nation of immigrants, built by immigrants, when that is not the complete truth, when we know certain kinds of immigrants have been embraced while other kinds of immigrants never were, have not been. And what could be more disrespectful and harmful to the lived spiritual and physical experiences of Native Americans and Black folks who have long been here, who done seen some things? Yes, I honor immigrants of every generation always, believe in immigrant rights for every generation always, but history also teaches us that America has assimilated European immigrants from every part of that continent with the singular mindset that they were White and that everyone else was not. So what could be more disrespectful than Chinese exclusionary laws or Japanese internment camps back then, or building a wall to keep out Latinx immigrants now? We say this is a melting pot, but for whom? Those European immigrants, then, now, who want to take a bite of the American pie, the American Dream, ultimately have to denounce anything else except Whiteness, and to participate in a culture, in a mindset, that speaks of that melting pot but really is about setting fire to anything that tells their history, their past, before they became White. When I address my White sisters and brothers, my White family, at speaking engagements, I ask them what they were before they became White. Most respond sheepishly about fragments of their family history, but, by and large, they know as little about their heritage as African Americans know about Africa, thanks to slavery and White supremacy. Yes, racism, White supremacy, wreaks havoc upon us all, equally. So gone, often, is the genius of, say, Irish culture, of Italian culture, of Polish culture, of Welsh culture, of French culture, and so on, replaced by Whiteness, White American culture, whose core is a legacy of theft and genocide and slavery and plunder and land-grabs and denial and hate and violence and fear in every imaginable form. In that context it is quite easy to understand why individuals like an Aaron Scott came so hard at my wife and me with that lawsuit, his political leanings notwithstanding. White American culture, as currently constructed, teaches and encourages people to behave this way, to blaze their path in the world recklessly, to crush everyone and everything in their way in order to get ahead. Because unfiltered and unchecked Whiteness, in this American context, is often absent of love, of forgiveness, of empathy, of compassion, of understanding the difference, say, between proactive anger and reactionary anger. This is why a Bobby Kennedy or an Eve Ensler are such beautiful human being examples. Bobby, then, understood that he needed to evolve, to grow, to heal, to not be what he was socialized to be, a spoiled and privileged White male in America. He needed to become a human being, with empathy, with compassion, with love, free to face all as his equal. The public execution of his brother and best friend, President John F. Kennedy, taught Bobby what suffering felt like, the same suffering dirt-poor Irish immigrants felt when they crawled on their bellies escaping the potato famine or found themselves crammed into New York and Boston ghettos. Bobby had to find himself, his humanity, in that American tragedy of his brother's lost life. And he did, and in his last years, could speak with and listen to any people anywhere. He had found his soul. And a human being, now, is what Eve Ensler is—one with the ability to listen and learn—and who is unafraid to challenge racism, White supremacy, sexism, homophobia and transphobia, eyeball to eyeball, with people of any background any time any place. Eve is a human being, with empathy, with compassion, with love, free to face all as her equal. Because Eve knows suffering, as a woman, as a Jewish woman, as a bisexual woman, as a cancer survivor, as that little girl who was brutalized by the childhood sexual violence of her father, and she has, miraculously, found it in her journey, in her art, in her play *The Vagina Monologues* and in her book *The Apology*, in her activism, in her life work, in herself, to love, to heal, to forgive, to empower others. In other words, White people who place Whiteness before their humanity face a humbling spiritual decision as America and this planet continue to be the multicultural world some of us are trying not to see: be a human being or be White. Moreover, Whites on the left must understand that they cannot be truly free unless they honor and respect people of color—all people of color—consistently, as human beings, as equals. Whites on the right must realize that they are not truly free if the foundation of their value system, whether they believe it to be Christian or not, is hate and fear of those who are not them, if they treat human beings not them as not being human, as not being equal. Whites in the middle, who like to call themselves moderates or centrists or neutral, need to know that fence-sitting never moves our nation or the human family forward. Either you support democracy and equality for all people, or you don't. Either you believe that we all belong to the human family—the human race—or you do not. There can be no middle ground when the lives of so many, across generations and centuries, across traumas and deferred dreams, have been sacrificed time and again on the altar of cowardice, because of blindness, because of political expediency, because of fear of change and fear of the future, because of a greedy lust for power and privilege, at any cost.

Yes, some of us will achieve great success in life, some of us will barely inch forward, some of us will get houses and cars and have careers and status, but the vast majority of us, be we working-class Whites in the mountains of West Virginia, or Mexican immigrants living in El Paso, Texas, or Black folks being gentrified out of major areas like Brooklyn, New York, or women fighting to control their bodies and battling for equal pay for equal work, or trans women warding off every effort to murder them—like for real—we all struggle for our lives and our collective wellness. Those who hold power but feel no love for the people thrive when the rest of us hate and fight each other... a reality as old as time itself. Therein lies the true measure of the tragedy of the Minnesota lawsuit and the ensuing media attacks. Those duped into believing that power works without love think that they can achieve power, or money, or status, or a career boost by ripping others apart. Look no further than any social media platform for proof positive of this mindset and behavior, for it is unapologetically toxic, and evil.

I say, more often than ever, that a day or week rarely goes by when I do not feel disappointment, disrespect, sadness, with us as Americans, as human beings. Whether in person or on social media, I see how people talk to—and at—me, and with each other, this entire culture of shredding people, of outing or canceling people, this "got ya" mentality, of not seeing anyone as a whole person, just pieces of a person, or just what we want to see. We go through life like soulless, programmed robots, far too many of us, and do not even realize it. As Marvin Gaye once sang, "this ain't livin'." Indeed, what it be is an existence that strips us of real freedom, of real democracy, of real humanity, of real people power, of real joy, and the end result is everything from daily and weekly gun violence, to horrific acts of sexual assault, to stupefying displays of bigotry and hate, to various forms of mental and spiritual illness. This is why I grimace and have such a difficult time swallowing what my mother still says to me as an adult because, in my pounding heart, I love her deeply, and I am so very clear that had my mother not risked her own life and her own safety I would not be who I am, I would not be alive, this I know. But I also know that I have a responsibility to myself, to this world, to whatever I believe in, to take the best parts of my ma and hold on to them for dear life; and to let go of the ugly parts, that I cannot be that part of my mother, that part of my family, that part of my community, or that part of America. I must continue to forgive my mother, yes, forgive my long absent and now dead father, yes, forgive the many people and many things that have so hurt me through the years, and to this day; I must forgive myself, over and over again, too, for every misstep, every walk backwards, I must I must I must, and

I will I will I will. And I must forgive this country, even as I challenge it every single day of my life. And it means, yes, I must forgive those people, in Brooklyn, New York, who got me arrested, and, yes, I must forgive those people in Minnesota, too, for the lawsuit, for the newspaper articles, for the hate-filled messages in the aftermath of those newspaper articles. Trust me I overstand, as we say, when I hear Black people, other people of color, Jewish people, Muslim folks, women of all backgrounds, LGBTQ+ folks, the disabled, poor people, people with dwarfism, detained immigrants, any who have ever been hated on, victimized, ostracized, marginalized, say they simply cannot forgive and forget. It has been excruciatingly difficult for my wife Jinah and I both not to feel anything but negative energy for those folks in Minnesota. But we both doubled down with therapy, with our spiritual practices, merely to get to a place of both forgiving ourselves and others. And I do in my heart believe we must practice love, and that love often cannot happen without forgiveness; but that forgiveness cannot occur if I, we, are not allowed to discuss our hurts, our traumas, what you, they, did to me, us. I do not believe in holding onto hurt and trauma forever, to holding grudges and gripes forever, but neither do I believe in blind forgiveness. Somehow and in some way, I humbly feel that real freedom comes for me, comes for us all, when we tell our truths, no matter how uncomfortable they may make other people feel. So, yes, I forgive those responsible for what happened to me, and I forgive myself for putting myself in any situations I could have and should have avoided. Because what purpose will be served by being angry and hurt for the rest of my life? *Hurt people also hurt themselves....*

I want to be free and I want us to be free, no matter who "us" is. As free as jazz giant Billy Taylor felt when he created the song "I Wish I Knew How It Would Feel to Be Free" in the 1950s. Mr. Taylor wrote that song when my mother was a young Black girl in the Low Country of South Carolina, in a region and a nation steeped in a form of legal and emotional and physical violence called Jim Crow, as "Whites Only" and "Coloreds Only" signs were hammered everywhere, including the tear-soaked walls of our shared history. Little did my mother know her education would be interrupted and stopped, permanently, by the eighth grade, because she had to work, because her family had inherited poverty and human degradation from previous generations, from the psyche and power trips of America. Little did she know that for the totality of her life she would battle racism, because she was Black, and sexism, because she was a woman, and classism, because she was poor. Little did my ma know that she would gather her few things, as many had done before her, and with two of her sisters migrate North searching for a better life, searching for freedom, in the wee hours of 1964, during the height of the Civil Rights Movement, just like immigrants are doing in this century. Little did my mother know that a few months after her arrival she would meet and fall in love with my father, that she would eventually give birth to me despite not being married to my father, and that she would be forced to raise me in the same savage poverty that she experienced in the American South, because my father was a sexist man, because he had been socialized to be a man who saw women as recycled sex toys and caretakers, and nothing more. Little did she know, as Janis Joplin once sang, that "Freedom's just another word for nothing left to lose." Little did my mother know that she would raise this boy, her man-child, to manhood, and that he would take the lessons and stories she shared with him again and again, and turn them into the passions of his life, to work for freedom and justice and equality for all people. Little did she know how much her son would suffer because of that work... how many times he would fall down, or get knocked down, trying to help himself, trying to help others, the way he had heard anonymous Black faces sing about these things in those spirituals she, his mother, taught him to love from birth. Yes, I do wish I knew how it would feel to be free, truly free, but when I left that Minnesota courtroom on that frigid December day, just like when I left that Brooklyn courtroom on that musty September afternoon, I knew that if I were ever going to be free, truly free, and if you, we, were ever going to be free, truly free, then it would have to begin in our minds, in our hearts, in our spirits, with the humble understanding that love, sweet love, would have to defeat hate; that forgiveness, gentle forgiveness, would have to defeat revenge; that empathy and compassion, heartfelt empathy and heartfelt compassion, would have to defeat the reckless disregard of each other; that action has to be the best friend of great ideas else the ideas mean nothing; that it is useless to say, over and over, that hurt people hurt other people, that as Pastor Mike Walrond in Harlem declares, covered people have to cover other people, that we must, well, help ourselves, and we must help each other; and that the sorrow songs we hum and deliver in this place called America will eventually have to be replaced by back-bending shouts of freedom as our souls are being born, again—

ABOUT THE AUTHOR

K evin Powell is one of the most prolific literary, political, cultural, and hip-hop voices in America. He is a poet, journalist, blogger, civil and human rights activist, public speaker, filmmaker, former two-time candidate for the United States Congress in New York City, and author or editor of 14 books. His writings have appeared in many different publications through the years, including *The Nation, British GQ, HuffPost, CNN,*
The Guardian, T: The New York Times Style Magazine,

The Washington Post, Vibe, Utne Reader, Ebony, Complex, African Voices, The Baffler, NPR, Esquire, The Progressive, and elsewhere. Kevin's critically acclaimed memoir, *The Education of Kevin Powell: A Boy's Journey into Manhood,* is being adapted for television. His next book will be a biography of Tupac Shakur, the global pop culture and hip-hop icon. As a speaker Kevin has lectured widely across America and internationally in places like Japan, the United Kingdom, and Nigeria, West Africa; he has also been a visiting scholar at several colleges, including Stanford University, Dillard University, and James Madison University. Kevin lives in New York City, the planet of Brooklyn.

ACKNOWLEDGEMENTS

I want to thank Ian Wallace and Hannah Wood at Apple Books for helping to give this little book life. I also want to thank my long-time editor Michael Cohen for his exceptional eyes; our art directors, Kerry DeBruce (front and back covers) and Hilary VanWright (interior of the book), for the stunning book design work; Michael Scott Jones, my friend and Alpha Phi Alpha Fraternity brother, for the equally beautiful cover photograph; Rodney Clancy, also a great art director, for the website; sound engineer Paul Arnold and production team The Cultural Bastards for the audio book recording; and David Young, my friend and Alpha Phi Alpha Fraternity brother, for suggesting the book title. Thank you as well to Nancy Prager of Prager Law and Edward Klaris and Alexia Bedat of Klaris Law for the legal support, and thank you to my publicist Billy Johnson, Jr., and my production assistant J.D. Wesley. Special salute to Todd Schuster and Jon Michael Darga at Aevitas Creative Management, and also my former literary agent there, Nick Chiles—you all have been a Godsend for me. Additionally, a special thank you to the young people on the cover of this book, for trusting me, my vision: Leila Tazi, Lylian Tazi, Juan Camilo Valencia, Nika Nunez, Shiv Masand, Victor Chen, Sophie Ming, Justin Dejesus Taveras, Sam Nielson, Iain

Nielson, Alexandra Jackman, Lexington Hardy, Kate Ke, Ellie Duebner, Annie Byrd, Juliette Bradley, Lucas Hegewisch. Likewise, many blessings to Dr. Jerry Ward, Ed Garnes, Dan Simon, Anthony Arnove, and Johnny Temple for giving me mad honest feedback on the various versions of this book. Finally, thank you to Miss Jinah Parker for being in my life, for all the invaluable lessons you have taught and re-taught me.

CPSIA information can be obtained
at www.ICGtesting.com
Printed in the USA
BVHW030214260122
627249BV00014B/177

9 781735 199726